UBUNTU

I AM BECAUSE WE ARE

By John Koelsch

UBUNTU, I Am Because We Are, 1st Edition.

ISBN 978-0-9896037-2-0 (e-book)
ISBN 978-0-9896037-3-7 (paperback)

LCCN 2019913651

www.brooklynwriterspress.com

www.johnkoelsch.com

CONTENTS

DEDICATION

This work was written first and foremost for my grandchildren and their children. I hope they will have a world to live in that will that will be better than the one we have now. I also wrote this for the rest of my family, my countrymen, and all *Homo sapiens* on this planet. My hope is we can see progress for everyone and establish governments that rule by the consent of the governed and not just the influence of the wealthy and powerful. This was the intent and hope of the founding father of the United States. We have not accomplished that intent.

At the heart of what they wished to accomplish was a society dedicated to universal equity, which would allow everyone to have the right to "Life, Liberty, and the pursuit of Happiness." While we have made some progress in that regard, we are woefully short of attaining it.

I ask myself, "How can I be happy if my brother and sister are unhappy?" This book is dedicated to all of you in the hope that you will understand and undertake the awesome task of leaving a better world for our children.

AUTHOR'S NOTE

Robert Kennedy once said, *"It's not sufficient just saying, 'Well I don't like the way things are going.' We have a responsibility to offer an alternative."*

Dear Reader,

First, let me note that I am from here and we are all in trouble. When I say I am from here, I mean I am a member of the species *Home sapiens*, indigenous to this planet. I also mean that all *Home sapiens* are in trouble.

We possess the means to destroy all life on this planet. We have been working on it for a very long time, under the delusion that we are protecting ourselves from one another. In that millennium-long process, we created organizations that feed and protect us, which quickly led to the formation of armies to fight other armies in order to conquer and rule, and not just survive. Empires rose, prospered, ruled and fell. We tried multiple approaches and always the same cycle and the same result.

This is especially troubling after establishing a government that is allegedly of the people, by the people, and for the people. I fear for the world my grandchildren will inherit, if they inherit anything at all. The United States has been a world leader for over a century, and yet we are now dysfunctional. So much so, that the current regime appears focused on two things. First, dismantling every program our government has created for the people, including healthcare, social security, environmental protection, and so on. Second, to divert every dollar possible to the wealthiest one percent and to corporations. This, while our country makes every effort to distance itself from its allies, and is embracing dictators and fascist regimes.

This book presents an alternative, albeit my alternative. It can change the structure of our government and allow us to get back on track in pursuit of a nation that is governed by the consent of the governed, which honors "Life, Liberty and the pursuit of Happiness" for all. It is a viable, bloodless and relatively peaceful alternative to effecting change at the national level.

We have consistently accepted the notion that electing better representatives is the answer. But electing better representatives will not make a significant impact in a system that is corrupted in ways that will not allow advancements to take place. We see blood and violence week-after-week that is driven by leadership aiming to divide and confuse, all the while, raiding the treasury without respect for law, decency or humanity. In short, the United States is changing for the worse. We need to re-establish our government as a functional organization that serves that delivers on the promise of our founding fathers.

The changes I propose can help correct our path and enable us, as a nation, to deal effectively with the problems we face. This change however may be the most difficult challenge ever faced by a country. It may prove tougher than a Civil War, a war to end all wars, and keeping nuclear power in check. But it is a change we must embrace, and to know where to begin we must first understand where we came from and how we got here. That is the purpose of this book. This book speaks a truth that needs to be heard, discussed and ultimately acted upon. I believe the truth it contains is the only non-violent path that will enable us to work effectively to save our country, ourselves and future generations to come.

I ask you to read it with an open mind and an open heart. I also ask you to respond with your thoughts and ideas about how to peacefully accomplish what needs to be done. You can contact me via my website at johnkoelsch.com if you would like to share your ideas with me.

Peace,

John Koeslch

PART 1

LEADERSHIP, REWARDS & CHALLENGES

THE JOURNEY TOWARD LEADERSHIP

"Leadership is not about being in charge and giving orders, or yelling and raving about desired results. A leader is simply someone who sees a situation, recognizes what needs to be done to achieve a desirable outcome and does what is required to achieve that result."

— TAC Officer

I was the second son born into a Roman Catholic family and the third child born from my mother's fourth pregnancy. Unlike my siblings, I was allowed and encouraged to explore the world and got by with little to no discipline. This allowed me the freedom to experiment and screw things up, and to examine things for what I saw them to be, and not for how I was told they were.

The Path of Religion

At the age of thirteen I left home to attend Divine Word Seminary and began my studies to become a Roman Catholic missionary priest. That year, I started to consider how I wanted my life to unfold and how I wanted to live it, which is not the same question as what I wanted to do. Eventually, I came to the conclusion that I wanted to live as a leader and guide people to achieve better results in order to lead more productive lives. By the time I was enrolled at Divine Word College I had come to two realizations. First, priests were not concerned with leadership, only control. Second, they had no clue how to help anyone live a better life; they only taught others how to comply with their views or face eternal punishment. It became obvious to me that the church was interested in the prosperity and advancement of the church far more than the salvation of a single soul. This would be my first encounter with the power of belief being utilized for the power to rule without any relevance to factual reality.

The Path of War

For a time, after leaving, I was rudderless, but I realized the predicament I was in. I was eighteen-years-old, not enrolled in an academic program, and subject to being drafted into a war I knew nothing about. I was fairly certain I did not want to be shot, so I enlisted for a non-combat assignment. And yet, through a series of small, seemingly inconsequential and unrelated decisions, I gave up my guaranteed non-combat assignment (in writing) and enrolled in Infantry Officer Candidate School. There I received my first real training on leadership.

To my good fortune, although I did not think so at the time, I was assigned to a platoon led by a TAC Officer who ignored us. All the other TAC Officers threatened and abused their candidates to discipline them into STRAC troops. They looked good. We did not. Horrible would be a kind word. Our TAC came around each week to give us enough demerits to eliminate any possibility of attaining weekend passes. We were a mess and we knew it. After six weeks, we demanded, pleaded redress. Our TAC, with deliberate meanness and pettiness, informed us we were stupid, ignorant and likely to expire badly in Southeast Asia. I still remember his words.

"Leadership is not about being in charge and giving orders, or yelling and raving about desired results. A leader is simply someone who sees a situation, recognizes what needs to be done to achieve a desirable outcome and does what is required to achieve that result. You are too stupid to understand this. Therefore, you will never be honor platoon because that ends in week-sixteen. However, at that point, you'll collectively wake up, and you'll be the best platoon in the company. Everyone will recognize that but you'll never be honor platoon. Now give me 500 push-ups and get out of my sight."

It would take ten weeks before the dawn would light up our brains. He was right. So precisely correct that it enabled me to receive my commission as a Second Lieutenant, Infantry. I was assigned a Basic Training Officer across the street from where I had trained. And I spent the next year learning about and struggling with the military's process for creating warriors. The military is both incredibly effective at producing a military machine and unrelentingly destructive to the individuals who experience it. The process works by demolishing individuality in unkind and occasionally wicked ways while creating a nearly overpowering commitment, or belief to being part of a greater cause. It works extremely well.

I took part and I struggled against this. It was an experience that could never affect change but did provide further insights into the mechanisms of leadership.

Then came Vietnam. I joined my platoon on April 22, 1968. My guiding ethos was "accomplish the mission and protect my men."

On May 5th, we were positioned just outside Saigon to intercept the Viet Cong and the North Vietnam Army. The second offensive, also known as Mini-Tet, had begun. It is considered to have been more aggressive and brutal than the January Tet Offensive for those fighting around Saigon.

For nine-days, I lead my men as we patrolled all day in what were called "Search and Destroy" missions, emphasis on destroy and ambushed all night.

May 1968, was the worst month of the entire war for American casualties, and I operated in one of the most intense areas. I lead my platoon, we killed the enemy, and many of our men were wounded. I lost three men wounded and was almost killed several times. We were gods of war and fought without mercy, and we won.

I continued to lead into the Third Offensive in August. Killing and death was the main sustenance. This included losing more men and getting wounded twice. It also included killing eight heavily armed enemy soldiers during an ambush one night and discovering in the morning that the oldest was maybe twelve, the youngest perhaps eight. This was "collateral damage." And it got worse, at my direction we began shooting, demolishing, and decimating the passengers on a yellow school bus because they drove into the trees at the Michelin plantation, at the wrong moment, and I made a mistake.

To protect my men, I also on three occasions, had my fully loaded M-16 set on automatic, pointed close distance at the belly of two of the men under my command, my Captain and my Colonel. I protected my men and didn't have to fire, but I was fully prepared to do so. I departed my assignment as Platoon Leader in Vietnam following my second Purple Heart. I can tell you all combat veterans of Vietnam brought the war home with them and have been paying for it ever since. It was not our fault, only our responsibility.

From that experience I formed a deep understanding for how teams work and a tremendous appreciation for the unintended consequences of leaders making decisions. This is especially true for arbitrary and capricious decisions, as well as, fully considered but ill-informed ones. And for small, seemingly inconsequential decisions and those decisions that impact the world.

I came home and went to college, intending to apply what I had learned about leadership to help people in the manner best suited to my skills and personality. I earned a B.A. in Political Science in three-years and a Master's of Public Administration in one-year through a Fellowship in the Southern Regional Training Program in Public Administration. Although I was driven and in a hurry to get to leadership, I still had so much to learn.

REAL WORLD LESSONS

"If your actions inspire others to dream more, learn more, do more and become more, you are a leader."

— John Quincy Adams

Over the next thirty-six years, I worked in the public sector at the state and local level with a great deal of interaction at the federal level. This period of my life helped me develop critical concepts around implementing effective decision-making, and supporting leadership growth through structural changes to teams. What I learned led to my having success with moving organizations toward better decision-making and leadership nearly everywhere I was employed. But I rarely stayed anywhere longer than four-years. This was in part due to my personal struggle with PTSD, as well as, the fact that I implemented what I had learned to the structure of these organizations. It seemed, time-and-again, my approach was always eagerly accepted at first and vehemently opposed shortly thereafter.

I share the following true stories from my experiences for two reasons. The first is so you understand that as difficult as it was back then, it was a breeze compared to accomplishing what I am proposing in this book. The second is so you can think about all of the difficulties this nation has experienced because the job did not get done forty-five years ago and ask yourself, "How bad will it be if we don't get it done now?"

In 2004, I retired on disability earned by my service in Vietnam.

Throughout my forty-four years of professional experience I learned a great deal about leadership, the impact of organizational structure, and the inherent strengths and weaknesses that impact a team's ability to accomplish their intended goals.

I've come to the conclusion that people really want change. They want things to be different, but they are unwilling to deal with change and are utterly opposed to it if they perceive it to be limiting to them personally.

The Kentucky Legislative Research Commission Internship

In 1972, while working as an intern for the Kentucky Legislative Research Commission through the Frankfort Administrative Intern Program, I had the privilege of being a quiet observer of the legislature's consideration in a Special Session of the proposed Equal Rights Amendment. My position allowed me to be present as a non-participant in every official meeting on the topic. As long as I sat quietly, I remained virtually unnoticed. I received a tremendous education in one week's time.

To set the stage, the state of Kentucky holds a regular legislative session for sixty-days every two years. An old Kentucky joke goes, "We would all be better off if they met two days every sixty years."

At this point, in 1972, the governor called a seven-day Special Session to consider two major issues and a half dozen minor ones. The minor issues could have waited, but they added political justification for calling the session. Politicians do not object to this type of tactic.

The two major issues were the Equal Rights Amendment to the Constitution and a major funding bill that was a key component of operating the state of Kentucky for the next two years. The bill had been passed in the previous regular session but had, in some inexplicable manner, been physically lost before the governor could actually sign it. It had to be passed again.

The Equal Rights Amendment was, of course, as toxic then as it is now. It was hotter than any southern barbecue and made people tipsy and devoid of their senses faster than the finest Kentucky moonshine. Once the proceedings commenced, the Equal Rights Amendment was considered first in the House of Representatives. Everyone knew it would pass and the real battle would be in the Senate. Nonetheless, people wanted to have their position on record and tensions were running high. I sat in the gallery on a balcony for observers set around the chamber.

The next day the House passed the Equal Rights Amendment, and it was sent to the Senate. The fun was about to begin. The Senate promptly referred the matter to committee. The committee convened at eight-thirty the next morning. I sat in the corner and watched. They promptly discovered that no one was willing to make a motion to discuss the bill, let alone act on it.

Senator Dee Huddleston, the majority leader who was running for the United States Senate, spent several hours discussing the matter, first with the chairman and then with each committee member.

The committee reconvened at eleven, and I sat in the same chair. The members stared at each other and sat silently; no one was willing to utter a word lest it be ruled as a motion to consider. They adjourned at twelve-thirty for lunch. Senator Huddleston conducted further conversations.

The committee reconvened at three. I sat in the same chair. I had a great view. I watched six members sit with lips sealed while the chairman pleaded, cajoled, and generally carried on about how they needed to do their patriotic duty. Silence ruled. They adjourned.

Amazingly, they reconvened at six. Senator Huddleston apparently could not force them to act, but he could make them sit in that room. Personally, I was finding my chair to be less than comfortable.

At seven they adjourned. The chairman then said, "This committee is called to order." An hour later he said, "This committee meeting is adjourned." In the interim, no one, including me, had said a single word.

The members left for the day. I hung around for a while because, as a quiet witness who was essentially a total non-entity in the matter, no one paid any attention to me. My instincts paid off, and I learned that Dee Huddleston was slated to have a conference that night with the Secretary of State.

My supervisor promised to call me with the results of that meeting no matter what time it was. I went home and sacked out with the phone only a few feet away.

At that time, the Kentucky Secretary of State was a woman named Thelma Stovall. She was a tough politician and extremely powerful in politics of the state. I figured that meeting would be fascinating and wished I could have been a quiet witness. It was clear there would only be two people in that room.

My phone blared out at three o'clock in the morning. The committee would meet at five, and the Equal Rights Amendment would be sent to the full Senate with no recommendation.

"How did Thelma make that happen? I asked.

My supervisor responded, "Apparently she simply told Dee that if he couldn't get the amendment on the floor for a vote, he couldn't be her United States senator. I'm not sure what he told the members of the committee, but it seems like it was effective."

I was in my chair promptly at five. The chairman convened the committee. Only the chairman and two other members were present. Words do not exist to describe the silence of the next five minutes.

Finally, the chairman slapped the table. He pointed to one member, "You make the motion."

The member mumbled, "So moved."

The chairman pointed at the other member. "You second the motion."

The member whispered, "Second."

The chairman, "All in favor, say aye."

One aye and two coughs were heard.

"All opposed, say nay."

It was silent for at least two milliseconds.

The chairman said, "With no opposition the motion passes. The bill goes to the floor for debate without any recommendation." He gaveled once. "Meeting adjourned."

The preamble was completed, and the battle was set to begin. The initial debate would be at one o'clock. It was to decide whether or not the bill should be voted on for final passage. There were three days left in the Special Session.

Debate continued all afternoon into the evening. Memorable moments included the inevitable warning by a very conservative senator that "As sure as we pass this bill, you know that somewhere in this state some damn, long-haired hippie will go into some restaurant and demand to use the women's bathroom."

Reactions to that comment ranged from laughter to derisive shouts of "shut up" or "sit down," and "that means more toilet paper in the men's room."

A black female senator gave an impassioned speech focused on how long this inequality would continue. While she gave a good speech, she blew it on a technicality. She referred to women as a minority. Several senators responded with comments such as, "More of you than there are of us." It was a fact determined by nature, not legislation that had nothing to do with equality but negated an otherwise fine speech.

Fascinating speeches continued into the evening but no one seemed to be persuaded to say much. There was a moment when one senator questioned the idea of women serving in combat. A shouted response of "What do you care? You're too chicken to serve!" shut him down.

They adjourned at seven. I went back to my supervisor to find out what was likely to happen. "Passage is in the bag. You'll see how the legislature really works." He explained the scenario.

I went home for the night and was back in the gallery when they opened the session at nine. The morning was taken up by more speeches, mostly silly. When the afternoon session began at one, the opponents fired their biggest gun.

They moved for adjournment *sine die*. The motion required no second, had to be voted on, and would shut down the Special Session without any other votes.

Senator Huddleston rose to speak. "Ladies and Gentlemen, this is very simple. We have not taken up the Expenditure Bill and we must pass it. If we fail to do so, portions of state government will shut down, the governor will be forced to call another very costly session, and the fallout from that will be on your heads. We must reject the motion."

Debate continued for some time, but in the end the motion failed. Several motions to consider the Expenditure Bill were shut down by the Majority Leader before a second was recognized. The Senate returned to the Equal Rights Amendment. Debate on that went on for several more hours. During this time Julian Carroll, the lieutenant governor, took the chair. There were thirty-eight senators and a vote of 19-19 would require Julian to cast the deciding vote.

The vote began. I had picked my spot carefully to be able to watch both Julian and a senator from western Kentucky. It was close. The senator I watched voted against the bill. The count was 20-18 against. Before anyone could blink, Julian hit the gavel and recognized the senator from western Kentucky. He rose and changed his vote to for the bill. The vote was 19-19. Julian had to decide. He rose to speak. He talked about courage and the necessity to man-up and vote.

"I believe there is a time to vote, and this is that time. I vote for the bill to be considered for passage," he thundered. He banged his gavel and sat down quickly. The vote for passage was scheduled for late the next day.

I was in my seat early, in position to watch Julian and another senator from the middle of the state. The opposition made numerous procedural motions to block the bill. All were futile.

The time came to vote on passage. Tension was high. Once the count was 19-19, it would be up to Julian to cast the deciding vote. Twice as quickly as the day before, Julian banged the gavel and recognized the senator I was keeping an eye on. That individual rose quickly and changed his vote. The Equal Rights Amendment had passed 20-18.

The first vote-changing senator reaped a significant political harvest and probably did well financially, if not getting the keys to Fort Knox. The second vote-changing senator reaped a tremendous political bounty and likely got the keys to Fort Knox for an overnight visit.

Julian Carroll ran for governor and was able to speak to ERA supporters and remind them that it was his vote that allowed the bill to be considered for passage. To opponents he was able to note blandly that he had no say in the actual passage.

He was elected governor. His tenure was marked by some financial inconsistencies. Dee Huddleston was elected United States senator from Kentucky, and he had a spectacularly undistinguished career in that position. Thelma Stovall served many more years and became lieutenant governor when Julian Carroll was governor. He was absent from the state when the legislature passed a resolution rescinding the Equal Rights Amendment. Thelma Stovall, as the acting governor, vetoed the resolution. In the end, the amendment fell three states short of the required thirty-eight state approvals for adoption.

The Tennessee Higher Education System

The Student Information System collected information on courses taken and demographics such as race, sex and marital status for evaluative purposes. It collected twenty-four separate items of information and was intended, combined with cost studies, to equitably finance 70% of all funding for public higher education. It utilized three of the items collected for funding reports and the rest of the information remained unused.

During the three-years under my operation it collected twenty-five items and utilized all of them for gaining a factual understanding for how the educational institutions operated and what they accomplished.

By my fourth-year, universities, colleges and community colleges were in need of structural changes, which coupled with a concern for whether or not funding levels could be maintained led to significant opposition to the use of the Student Information System. This became a highly charged political issue, in part because it involved, Tennessee State University—a historically black university. The legislature chose to disregard the System's factual reporting, and began to dismantle it after approving increased funding for all. I chose to leave.

Town Infrastructure

As Town Administrator for a town with a population of about five-thousand people I implemented a program seeking development grants from the state. My Board members were opposed to this, as they were convinced they could never receive a grant from the state. I pleaded with them to allow me to proceed with the program and within the first two years was able to bring in 2 million dollars to implement needed infrastructure improvements. The program would produce over 10 million dollars in its first five-years and even after my departure it continued to run in my absence.

A Strategic Budget Process

As a City Manager, I designed, developed and successfully implemented the Strategic Budget Process. At the time it was the only systematic program in existence for implementing comprehensive decision-making into budget decisions, which determined how organizations would ultimately operate.

In August 1993, the International City Management Association published a Management Information System Report on my process. I was informed it sold over 5,000 copies and became the third best-selling MIS Report produced at the time. It was eventually abandoned because politicians are inherently uncomfortable making factual decisions concerning operations.

UBUNTU

"Ubuntu speaks of the very essence of being human. We say "Hey, so-and-so has ubuntu." Then you are generous, you are hospitable, you are friendly and caring and compassionate. You share what you have. It is to say, "My humanity is caught up, is inextricably bound up, in yours." We belong in a bundle of life. We say, "A person is a person through other persons."

— Desmond Tutu, No Future Without Forgiveness

I first came across the word *ubuntu* in a Facebook meme. A man working with children in Africa proposed a race for which the winner would win candy. He set the children in line and hollered "one, two, three, go!" The children, after joining hands raced to the finish line, and crossed it together. All of them were awarded candy, but the man perplexed by their behavior asked them, "Why did you choose to run that way?"

One child responded, "How could I be happy if my brother or sister is unhappy?"

Then the man understood, "*ubuntu.*"

In the Xhosa culture, the word *ubuntu* is used as a greeting and translates to "I am because we are." It is meant as a reminder of the essential facts of our humanity, which is that we are all on the same boat and should behave accordingly. Generally, this is not how we behave. *Homo sapiens* are a combative species that tend to be more concerned with taking over the boat than sharing it, but why?

Why are we so ready to harm, even kill, others without any valid justification? Why do we glorify war as a noble thing in and of itself? Why do we hold substantial reluctance over helping people if we perceive them to be different or somehow less worthy? Why do we care about some people, and not all people? At the heart of these questions is another, who are we? Why do we not all live by *ubuntu*? Of course, the answer is complex.

Consider how a species without fangs or claws or poison, of relatively small stature and strength, without speed or camouflage, could come to protect itself and survive, let alone dominate the planet?

Ubuntu! The question of who we are lies in the 'we.' No one person got here by him or herself. Only by working together as a team, we survived. As a team, we ate better, and grew stronger. Our dietary changes enlarged our brains and enabled us to think bigger and better. We became empowered as a team to create. We created language to communicate. We created tools, learned how to use fire, how to track and hunt prey and how to make art. We gained an appreciation for what was available beyond what was in front of our eyes. We developed a reliance on memory, and the ability to plan for the short and long-term. The next meal in the short-term, and shelter, food and survival needs for the long-term. We evolved, and the experience of living improved, so how did we end up in the mess we are in?

At this writing, there are over 7.3 billion people living on this planet. In 1900, there were approximately 1.6 billion, and some projections today estimate that by 2100 that number will increase to 11 billion. It took us approximately twelve-thousand years to grow from 4 million to 1.6 billion. Our planet, if properly managed and maintained, could potentially support the projected population increase and replenish itself, but as evidenced by climate change, we have not been doing a good job. The proven fact is that 95% of climate change is man-driven. We have been depleting and destroying, not nurturing or maintaining.

The level of nourishment and consumption of resources we are accustomed to in this country is far higher than a significant portion of the rest of the world. It is estimated that 1 billion people are starving to death and another billion are seriously undernourished. Coal and oil have become scarce and are harder to access, and yet we minimize the worth of alternative energy sources because they could reduce potential profits for energy-producing conglomerates, and would require a change in our lifestyle. It is difficult to determine how much our planet can replenish itself given the trend toward an increasing population.

In 2018, what the United States could look back on was a century of war, with an estimated death toll exceeding 7.2 million. Plagues and natural disasters killed even more. Worse still, our own creativity has enabled us to develop weapons that can destroy human life, and potentially all human life, by our own direct actions. We are standing on the precipice of a world-ending nuclear war or other potential 'world-killing' disasters. If we do not figure out how to provide food, shelter and healthcare for everyone, the number of people dying in this century will be staggering. With the human race seemingly focused on gaining power and financial gain by any means necessary, the solutions to our population dilemma are Malthusian.

Over the course of human history, our leaders have enabled the formation of tribes, kingdoms, empires and modern-day states. However, there is a critical problem inherent in all human organization, and it is best defined by how we fail and how we succeed when we work together. Add to this the impact of past and current leadership, how religion has been tied to it, and remains one of the strongest forces in human society. In the 'we' the challenges we face are clear to see.

We performed admirably and now dominate the planet. But the 'we' who dominates now, is some of us, not all of us. Still the burden remains with all of us to figure out how to reset our nation's course as set forth by our founding fathers.

A NEW KIND OF COUNTRY

"We must all hang together,
or assuredly we shall all hang separately."

— Benjamin Franklin, Signing of the Declaration of Independence

Following the end of the Revolutionary War, our founding fathers were faced with the task of creating a new country. They proposed something that had never been seen before: a government governed by the consent of the governed, and a joint commitment to pursuing, life, liberty and happiness for all.

They knew they could not hold everyone together with the Articles of Confederation. It is relatively easy to get people to gang up and fight a war. But not so easy to persuade them to live together as friends and neighbors and be reasonably peaceful about it.

"They called a meeting of all of the colonies which they named the Grand Convention or the Federal Convention because if they called it the Constitutional Convention to draft a document to run a nation, they were pretty sure about two-thirds of states won't show up. Fifty-five Delegates from twelve states attended. Rhode Island threw a snit fit and was not there."

"They had a tough nut to crack to resolve all of the different opinions and deal with issues real and issues just passing through. They managed to do it by setting out a process and whenever it didn't work, ignoring it."

— The Miracle At Philadelphia by Catherine Dinker Bowen

Some of the things they needed to figure out included:

Should government be federal or national?

That is, should they focus on the operation and interaction of the states, who have all created their own system of governing, and should they work to ensure amicable operations between them? Or should they focus on a complete and compulsive operation, supporting individuals and directing states on the path they should take?

The question of two supremes

What is to happen when the supreme authority of the nation and the supreme authority of the state do not agree? Who must surrender to whom? A fellow named Gouverneur Morris from Pennsylvania had a pithy comment to add on that:

"When the powers of a national government clash with the states, only then must the states yield."

"We had better take a supreme government now than a despot twenty years hence, for come he must."

— The Miracle At Philadelphia by Catherine Dinker Bowen

The Head of a Nation

Deliberations on federal vs. national naturally lead to the consideration of how a head of a nation is chosen—appointed or elected—and by whom? No king is strongly supported, but proposals for 'Head' range from powerful limited single-person to dual leadership and triumvirates. Also of concern was how long someone could remain as head.

Veto Power

The question of who can veto whom and how and about what best defines who has the power to do what?

Legislative Representation

Following close on the heels of head of state is how states will be represented in the legislature? And whether they are appointed or elected and by whom? The arguments extend to fair representation for smaller states to they are not overpowered by higher population states. Many delegates were suspicious of the people due to Shay's Rebellion so there was continuing discussion around who should be allowed to vote? This Rebellion against local taxation led to the Constitutional Convention, which was charged with repairing the Acts of Confederation. It also raised serious doubts about allowing the average man to vote.

Roger Sherman proposed a compromise on the legislature with an upper and lower house. Each state would get one representative with one vote in the upper house and multiple representatives based on population in the lower house. Sherman's compromise looked like the most workable solution, but it had a long way to go.

Once you start basing representation on population, you have to count the population which raises the question of whether or not slaves count. It was proposed that "The vote should be in proportion to the whole number of white and other free citizens and three-fifths of all other persons except Indians not paying taxes." (The Miracle At Philadelphia by Catherine Dinker Bowen) "All other persons" were of course slaves, a word carefully excluded from the Constitution.

Another proposal was to base the vote in the lower house according to "quotas of contribution." This meant it would be according to taxes paid and the tribute each state brought into the national treasury. But what about slaves?

Elbridge Gerry from Massachusetts interposed, "Blacks are property and are used to the southward as horses and cattle to the northward. Why then should not horses and cattle have the right of representation in the North?" (The Miracle at Philadelphia by Catherine Dinker Bowen.)

People's Consent

The idea that must hold above all others must be that of the people consenting and agreeing.

Citizenship

The need to define the requirement of citizenship for holding national office. Many foreigners had fought to free America and indeed were integral to the success of that effort. Should they now be denied a chance to serve in the government because they are of French or English origin? The answer must be yes for the chief executive. For senators and representatives, flexibility was allowed.

Three Parts of Government

The executive, legislative and judicial divisions made up the core of the system of government in plan-after-plan. Further, they needed to define treason, determine the seat and extent of taxing powers, and establish the proportion of representatives from state to state. Working out these myriad details could change the United States from a confederation into a workable, lasting federal republic.

From May to September of 1787, ideas were proposed, debated, argued, dismissed and re-considered. Compromises were reached. Slowly a new nation emerged. Near the end of negotiations, the final and perhaps most important part of the puzzle was brokered. It simply stated that whenever two-thirds of Congress deemed it necessary, the Constitution could be amended after ratification of three-fourths of the states.

The Convention adopted the Constitution on September 17, 1787. Ten amendments known as The Bill of Rights were added by Congress when ten states had approved the Constitution.

The deliberations of the Constitutional Convention had been held in strict secrecy. Anxious citizens gathered outside Independence hall when the proceedings ended to learn what had been produced behind closed doors. The answer was provided immediately. A Mrs. Powel of Philadelphia asked Benjamin Franklin, “Well, Doctor, what have we got, a republic or a monarchy?” Without any hesitation whatsoever, Franklin responded, “A republic, if you can keep it.”

THE GROWTH OF A NEW NATION

"The soldier above all others prays for peace, for it is the soldier who must suffer and bear the deepest wounds and scars of war."

— Douglas MacArthur

In 1789, the French had a revolution of their own. They resolved this with a coup d'état and in 1798 called on Napoleon Bonaparte, a military hero to protect their new government. He promptly overthrew them and formed a dictatorship that would last until 1815.

Despite President Washington taking the stance of neutrality in regard to external conflicts, both Britain and France wanted the United States to pick sides. France had been a key ally in winning our independence, but trade with Britain was a key element of economic importance to a growing nation. The basic exigencies of politics played out at a full-scale symphony when American shipping took a hit from both France and Britain. The latter's interference lead to an unpopular settlement known as Jay's Treaty.

The Spanish meanwhile had their own challenges to contend with and ceded the territory of Louisiana to Napoleon, who was busy with his own wars and did not consolidate control. President Jefferson decided to purchase Louisiana and as much of Florida as we could gain. Before he could make an offer, Napoleon suggested America purchase it for fifteen million dollars. And although Jefferson considered the purchase was likely to be unconstitutional he presented it to Congress. They approved the purchase and America experienced its first major expansion.

Both Britain and Spain claimed previous rights to portions of the newly acquired territory. What followed were shipping raids and Britain's declaration of war on the United States in 1812. War went as wars go. Some battles were won, some were lost. Washington was captured, the White House burned, Napoleon defeated Europe, The Treaty of Ghent was signed in 1814, and the British were defeated at the battle of New Orleans in 1815. Meanwhile, a group of Federalists convened at Hartford and discussed secession from the Union, which did not happen at that point in time.

Then America experienced the Era of Good Feeling from 1815 to 1825, despite its first financial collapse in 1819. Recovery from the collapse proceeded until a major economic, political and moral issue broke out. The importation of slaves had been abolished by the Constitution in 1808, but slaves had become overwhelmingly important to the economy of the southern states. At the time, political power had been evenly divided between eleven 'free' and eleven 'slave' states, when Missouri, a 'slave' state, requested admittance into the Union.

Immediate dissension followed the disruption of the political balance and posed a threat to the economy. Questions about the morality of slavery pushed to the forefront. A compromise was reached by essentially splitting Missouri into a half-free, half-slave state. The Union held together for some time.

By 1820, the western expansion of the United States had pushed to the Mississippi River and displaced many Native American tribes. The Indian Removal Act was introduced by the hero of New Orleans, and Andrew Jackson created the infamous 'Trail of Tears.' In 1835, a war with Mexico resulted in Mexican rule being overthrown. And finally, Texas, a slave-state saw a tremendous influx of American settlers, and its slow admittance to the Union was finalized in 1845.

The pressures of expansion and the issue of slavery continued to build, and by the election of 1860, many southern states saw secession as inevitable if Abraham Lincoln was elected president. He was elected and South Carolina was the first to secede, followed by seven other states. Violent encounters with blood and death occurred with increasing frequency, but the conflict officially began in April 1861 and rapidly expanded to a full-scale war after Confederate troops opened fire on Fort Sumter, South Carolina.

The South had a great military tradition with some of the finest generals, including Robert E. Lee, Joseph Johnston, and Stonewall Jackson. Most of the fighting happened on home turf and the South only needed to survive to win the war. The North had the greater economic engine, an indomitable leader committed to preserving the Union, as well as, the moral imperative of ending slavery, although that was not the war's major purpose. Lee surrendered to Grant on April 9, 1865.

This was the most brutal war fought on the North American continent, with an estimated total number of casualties ranging from six-hundred-thousand to eight-hundred-thousand. Its impact rings still in the present day despite the appeal of President Lincoln to "bind up the nation's wounds." The United States has never completely healed from this war.

Expansion continued with the America-Indian War until 1890, which ended with the defeat of the great tribes of the plains. The United States covered the continent "from sea to shining sea."

In 1897, a minor excursion known as the Spanish-American War included a declaration of war, a short period of fighting, and the signing of the Treaty of Paris to end hostilities but never amounted to much.

The twentieth century dawned with a commitment to growth and a sense of wonder as to what was to come. By 1914, America had built the Panama Canal. Great railroads crisscrossed across the country. Airplanes, after having been demonstrated feasible by the Wright Brothers in 1903 had begun climbing to their place in commerce, and the world was bright with a surge in inventions. Then it happened, a century of promise became a century of war.

World War I

In 1917, the US entered World War I, the Great War. The war to end all wars. Inevitably it led to the next war. Total estimated number of deaths worldwide: 18,424,322

World War II

In 1941, it was World War II. The world at war with atrocities never before seen, ended with entry into a world with nuclear weapons. However, this did not end war either. We helped Europe recover and moved on to yet another war. Total estimated number of deaths worldwide: 48,231,700

Korea

In 1950, we visited the "Frozen Chosin" in Korea. The forgotten war that paused with a truce that is still in place. Total estimated number of deaths: 1,200,000

Vietnam

In 1955, we intervened in Vietnam. Officially the war ran from 1965 to 1973. As it turns out, we spent as much effort fighting ourselves as we spent on Charlie. No truce this time. No victory either, although we declared victory and left. Total estimated number of deaths: 3,900,000

Cold War

We paused and kept ourselves busy with the Cold War. No casualty estimates.

Gulf War

In 1990, the Gulf War, sometimes referred to as "now you see me, now you don't," occupied 100 hours. Total estimated number of deaths: 100,000.

Afghanistan

In 2001, we decided to top the record for Russia's longest war and entered Afghanistan. We broke their record, and Afghanistan now holds the record for our longest war. Total estimated number of deaths: 149,000 and counting.

Iraq

In 2003, we invaded Iraq; stumbling into war, we fought hard and well, and once again declared an unrealized victory and left. Total estimated number of deaths: 251,000.

In 2019, we look back on a century of war and the total estimated number of deaths: 72,256,022. The twentieth century has greeted American with numerous amazing and terribly unpleasant experiences. We recovered from a depression and created social security. We rebuilt Europe and led the world to a fantastic period of economic growth. President Kennedy was assassinated, and we fulfilled his dream of landing on the moon and returning home safely. Technology created the Internet and changed the way the world communicates. We unleashed the power of the atom on Hiroshima and Nagasaki, and we have managed, so far, not to destroy our planet.

The survival of the Republic is more uncertain today than it was in 1860. We have not learned to live in peace with one another, let alone with the rest of the world.

PART 2

THE COMPLEXITY OF TEAMS, I AND WE

THE MISSION OF 'WE'

*"Teamwork is the ability to work together
toward a common vision.
The ability to direct individual accomplishments
toward organizational objectives.
It is the fuel that allows common people
to attain uncommon results."*

— Andrew Carnegie

What is the difference between a team and a mob? The difference lies in leadership and the goals they persuade others to follow. Both, teams and mobs require the union of two or more people working in concert toward a unified goal. Teams tend to be made up of people working together and supporting one another. Mobs tend to be made up of groups of people who are often drawn together by lawlessness, disorder and ill intention.

The saying, "There is no I in TEAM" is not exactly correct. A team, at least a highly functional one, consists of more than one 'I.' And every member must commit to the goals of the 'we' if the intended goals are to be achieved. As we've clearly seen, there are numerous negative consequences when there is a divergence away from the mission of the 'we.'

How has the fact that *Home sapiens* are a team species worked for us? Well, we have survived —so far. We have dominated this planet as no other species ever has. We have even taken our first tentative steps to spreading our existence into other worlds. Not too bad, considering the signs that future extinction is possible.

Think not?

The Issue of Resource Depletion

I grew up in a small city in northern Ohio on the shores of Lake Erie, a small member of the Great Lakes, which contain 21% of the world's surface fresh water by volume. After fishing proved to be severely depleted, and recreational swimming was considered inadvisable and potentially hazardous, Lake Erie was dubbed the Dead Sea. And in 1969, the Cuyahoga River, which flows through Cleveland, Ohio into Lake Erie caught fire, not once, but twice. The cause of these fires was attributed to the oil slicks from steel mills and factories which resulted in spontaneous combustion.

In those days, little attention was paid to pollution. However, a positive outcome driven by the 'We' and due in part to these incidents, was the adoption of the Clean Water Act over the veto of Richard Nixon. It is considered to be one of the most effective environmental programs ever implemented and today the river and Lake Erie are cleaner than they used to be. This proves we can make progress toward resolving the environmental problems that stem from the way we have industrialized our world without a consideration for possible consequences. The depletion of resources is without question a culprit that leads to negative, unintended side effects.

In February 2017, our president signed an executive order inciting a process to repeal the Clean Water Act and replace it with a set of regulations that would substantially weaken the regulations.

Still debating the signs of future extinction?

1 billion people on this planet are starving and another billion are undernourished. The rest of us are okay, right?

Or are we?

Well, we mostly have enough to eat. But what are we eating? Poultry and beef that is injected with hormones, that are impacting us in ways that are not yet clearly defined. Have you noticed lately the cans of vegetables on grocery store shelves labeled non-GMO? This means, they are grown from seed that has not been genetically modified. Again, we have not yet been able to define the impact of genetic modification? Combined with the ongoing depletion of resources from our oceans, there is no guarantee that these methods will ensure an adequate food supply for the future.

Another example is evident in the oil industry. Oil is a non-renewable resource, which means once it's gone, there will be no more for millions of years. British Petroleum's estimate relies heavily on proved reserves. This is a method of calculating how much drillable oil we know is underground. The planet has 53.3 years of oil left at the current rate of production, according to BP's annual statistical review of world energy. Just 53 years! According to the report, the total number of identified oil reserves reached 1,687.9 billion barrels at the end of 2013, sufficient to meet the 53.3 years of global production. (British Petroleum Report, July 9, 2014)

Do you think in the next half-century alternative energy sources will be sufficiently advanced and available to keep our world fueled without oil? Consider 'proved coal' with an estimated world supply of 150 years. We need to consider whether or not it is a viable alternative to oil.

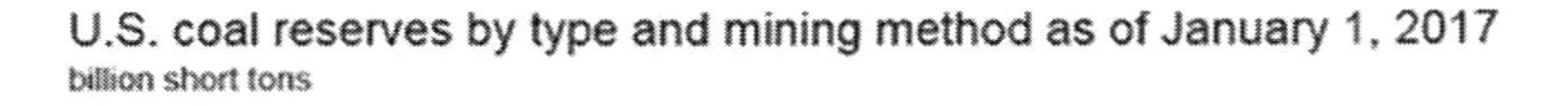

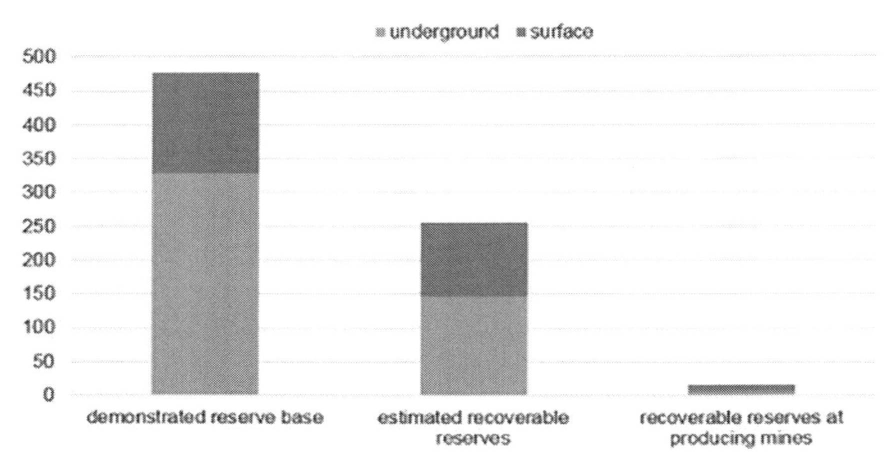

Source: U.S. Energy Information Administration, *U.S. Coal Reserves*, Table 15, November 2017 

As we face an increase in the world's population of over 20% in the next 82 years, we can't ignore the potential effects of pollution. Especially the environmental damage that can result from the use of coal to attain the food to feed ourselves, the energy to heat our homes, and all of the necessary resources to support society. Finally, consider the approach of our world leaders. Some are trying, but our president has withdrawn us from the environmental accords we previously supported. Those accords represent an extremely marginal approach to the issues that can likely define our extinction. And as we know, extinction happens to a species when it outgrows or fails to adapt to its changing environment. It is not an overnight event.

While many would argue that we will not die from a lack of food and energy, that is probably true, more likely, we will kill each other while fighting over these issues. Our leadership has led us to develop the nuclear bomb, which provides the means by which to wipe human life off of this planet. The president has recently withdrawn us from the Intermediate Range Nuclear Weapons Treaty (INF.) A treaty Russia has been violating for years. We are now, once again, plunging into a race to develop more and better nuclear weapons with which to destroy ourselves.

The dinosaurs could not do much about their extinction, whether it was a huge meteor from space, a volcanic action from the earth itself, or any other combination of events because they could not see it coming.

We, by contrast, are working toward our extinction, an extinction for which 'we' are the sole cause. We can clearly observe its approach. We can begin to prevent it, or we can smile and journey merrily along to the end. It depends on the team, which depends on its leaders.

THE STRUCTURAL COMPLEXITY OF TEAMS

"It is the beginning of wisdom when you recognize that the best you can do is choose which rules you want to live by, and it's persistent and aggravated imbecility to pretend you can live without any."

– Wallace Stegner, All The Little Live Things

The greater the goals and the more extensive the purpose of the team, the more complex the mechanisms of the team in terms of structure. In society, the mechanism of control meant to prevent chaos and team failure is law. In corporations, the same can be accomplished by way of rules and regulations.

Together, laws, rules, and regulations are aimed at creating the structural balance that allows teams to perform and function effectively. Those who enforce these laws, rules and regulations create them for their own reasons and typically tie them to their held position of power. This in turn results in overriding team goals.

As a society, we innately accept laws, rules and regulations even when they go against our intentions and desires simply because this is the way things are and the way they have always been. After all, it is the team structure that has allowed humans to dominate on this planet. So, we reason, if laws, rules and regulations exist, they must be necessary to our survival. This is mostly true when they work as intended. This is not the outcome when laws are poorly prescribed or utilized to attain individual power over attainment of shared team objectives.

Those wishing to maintain power under the guise of leadership often do so by keeping their cabals in line and to utilize a team's structure to retain both power and control. Simply put, you need not argue over whether an intended action is good or bad if the laws allow you to control or prevent a certain action. In this way, the control of an organizational structure become the only determining factor as to which actions are to be taken and which prevented.

Presidential Nominations

This can best be demonstrated by taking a closer look at how we handle presidential nominations to the Supreme Court. In a presidential nomination to the Supreme Court there are two ways in which structure can be controlled to achieve to possible outcomes.

To prevent a nomination from being considered, control of the structure can lead to disallowing a hearing from ever occurring. When the aim is to force a presidential nomination to begin, control of the structure leads to beginning the approval process without ample time for review or sufficient knowledge of the candidate's background. A hearing and subsequent vote is then required to take place. This goes to show that structure can obviate, even the highest, most committed leadership. It leads to the creation of a team within the greater team, one that is in pursuit of its own self-serving initiatives. These kinds of teams are much more difficult to define and identify, and are immeasurably more difficult to bring under control.

A Team's Structural Complexity

Whether you supported it or not, the entire Obama presidency had to struggle every step of the way against a structure controlled by those interested only in power and their own prosperity. If you opposed Obama's presidency, you might think, "Good! We won." That is not an unexpected reaction, but consider that those who held control over the structure had no concern for you. And in the future, others will inevitably control that structure and the direction they choose to take will once again hold little regard for what is most important to you.

That said, I am referring to more than political opposition. I am referring to those who bought and paid for the actions taken by that opposition. The oligarchy—the corporations and the wealthy 1% who run our country. The structure, if being used to attain and maintain power, can easily be bought.

A team's structural complexity depends on its size, its goals, the diversity of the challenges it faces and the strength of its leadership. Based on these defined criteria, the federal government of the United States is probably the most complex team on this planet. If we allow structural control to continue to be the deciding factor in all of the important decisions of our federal government, then we have no control, and we have no democracy. When we have no say in decision-making we don't even have a country.

I am fully in favor of extensive analysis and an extended open debate over what the decisions should be. For a chance to pursue a "Life, Liberty and the pursuit of Happiness" a country must be governed by the consent of the governed. If each citizen does not partake in a share of prosperity, no-one will prosper for very long. If our country is not to end, then we must all take responsibility for putting it back on track toward achieving the goals our founding fathers envisioned.

THE 8 BENEFITS OF TEAMWORK

"Individual commitment to a group effort—that is what makes a team work, a company work, a society work, a civilization work."

— Vince Lombardi

1st Benefit: Shared Labor

The first benefit of teamwork is shared labor. Whether voluntary or coerced, the sharing of labor expands what is possible to accomplish, and exceeds well beyond what one can do by him or herself.

The Giza Pyramids were built to endure an eternity and are doing just that. The monumental tombs are relics of Egypt's Old Kingdom era and were constructed 4,500 years ago. Egypt's pharaohs expected to become gods in the afterlife. To prepare for the next world, they erected temples for the Gods and massive pyramid tombs for themselves that were filled with the things each ruler would need to guide and sustain life after life.

Pharaoh Khufu's first Giza pyramid began around 2550 B.C. His Great Pyramid is the largest in Giza and towers some 481 feet (147 meters) above the plateau. It is estimated to have been constructed by 2.3 million stone blocks, each weighing an average of 2.5 to 15 tons.

Khufu's son, Pharaoh Khafre, built the second pyramid at Giza, circa 2520 B.C. His necropolis included a Sphinx, likely to stand sentinel for the entire tomb complex. It is a mysterious limestone monument with the body of a lion and a pharaoh's head. The third of the Giza Pyramids is considerably smaller than the first two, but it featured a more complex mortuary temple. It was built by Pharaoh Menkaure circa 2490 B.C. Each massive pyramid is but one part of a larger complex, including a palace, temples, solar boat pits, and other features. (National Geographic. Pyramids of Giza by Bran Handwerk)

Estimates on the size of the workforce required to complete these projects range from ten-thousand to thirty-thousand. The engineering and assembly is so complex, modern scientists have not yet figured out how they did it. It is certain that those aspects of the project were not the work on one man.

2nd Benefit: Support

In teamwork getting support from others as needed is often derived from less regarded members of the team. When you consider projects even greater than building the pyramids, such as landing a man on the moon, it becomes apparent that the coordination of multiple efforts is what is required to achieve a positive outcome. These efforts may include manual labor and intellectual capital such as, mathematics, engineering, and computer development.

According to an article in Smithsonian magazine, as America stood on the brink of a second World War, the push for aeronautical achievement grew ever greater and spurred an insatiable demand for mathematicians. A demand for which the best solution was women who were ushered into the Langley Memorial Aeronautical Laboratory in 1935 to shoulder the burden of number crunching.

Langley, a research complex, was built in 1917 and was the headquarters for the National Advisory Committee for Aeronautics (NACA) which was intended to turn the floundering flying gadgets of the day into war machines. In the decades before the digital age, the population of sharp and successful women at Langley skyrocketed. They acted as human computers, and freed up engineers from making hand calculations. Many of these 'human computers' are finally getting their due, however conspicuously missing from the story of female achievement are the contributions by courageous African American women, aka the West Computers after the area to which they were relegated. The West Computers were at the heart of the center's advancements as they helped blaze a trail for mathematicians and engineers of all races and genders to follow.

They worked through equations that described every function of the planes, and they ran numbers, often without a sense for the greater mission of the project. Despite this they made significant contributions to the ever-changing design of a menagerie of wartime flying machines by making them faster, safer and more aerodynamic. Some of these women after demonstrating stellar abilities were allowed to leave the computing pool to work on specific projects. Christine Darden worked to advance supersonic flight and Katherine Johnson calculated trajectories for the Mercury and Apollo missions.

NASA shut down the operations relying on the work of human computers in the 1970s as a result of technological advancements making their work obsolete. (Smithsonian magazine. "The True Story of 'Hidden Figures.' The Forgotten Women Who Helped Win The Space Race." September 8, 2016)

3rd Benefit: Diversity

This includes a diversity of analysis, perspective and intellect needed to resolve issues. Athens which is the largest of Greece's city-states is a great example of this.

The concept of democracy, which means 'rule of the people' was introduced in Greece after the Pisistratid Dynasty ended. It meant equality for all, except for slaves and women, of course. A triumvirate group government was created and included the Areopagus, an aristocratic council with a great amount of money and power, the Council of the Five Hundred, made up of an elected group of people with some money and power, and the Ecclesia or Assembly which included everyone else excluding slaves and women. An arena for debate was set up and different from anything humans had tried before. Democracy, among other things, enabled the greatest philosophers in history to set forth their ideas.

Socrates' beliefs on truth and wisdom laid the groundwork for Western systems of logic and philosophy. Sentenced to death after being found guilty of refusing to acknowledge the gods recognized by the state, and for corrupting youth by advocating a philosopher king government over democracy, he drank hemlock. Socrates honored the concept of team over individual and believed his death would quiet the dispute over governance. In this way, the city could be calmed before it split itself apart. He also, at the cost of his life, demonstrated the hazards of publicly disputing those in power.

Plato, a student of Socrates, founded the first institution of higher learning in the Western world known as the *Academia*, the Academy in Athens.

Aristotle, among his many accomplishments argued that the state is in fact much more than the local union for the prevention of wrong-doing and the convenience of exchange or an institution of protection for the gods and property. The true potential of the state was for it to become a genuine moral organization for developing the advancement of humans. This idea was truly unique and marvelous but never fully implemented. What we're left with is two dominant forms of human government, democracy and dictatorship. With the latter being the less successful, especially for those who live under it.

4th Benefit: Shared Prosperity

A rising sea lifts all ships. This bit of conventional wisdom works well for actual ships in actual ocean harbors, but is not quite as equitable when applied in terms of human economies. Income inequality is an ongoing concern in our country and throughout much of the world.

Generally speaking, successful enterprises do create some amount of shared prosperity. For example, Apple, Microsoft and Amazon made their founders wealthy beyond the dreams of Midas. One could argue that in this way, the prosperity of these corporations did in fact raise many other ships with their rising tide.

When it comes to human governance we need to take into consideration how to best increase the experience of shared prosperity among our global population. And in this way address the issues of income inequality, as well as, social issues concerning access to food, clean water and other needed resources.

5th Benefit: Individual Assets

In a high functioning team, members are encouraged to contribute whatever assets they possess. The success of team is essentially enabled by individual contributions and accomplishments that lead to expanded opportunities.

For example, Microsoft and Apple did not create the World Wide Web that made their work so successful and facilitated the expanded use of computers in homes and corporate settings. Facebook and the many applications that followed were again the result of those who made it possible for computers to access the internet. Further success by any of these companies could only be born from an earlier success of those who introduced a vehicle or medium for the masses to participate.

6th Benefit: Group-Powered Commitment

I refer to this as the 'Rah Rah!' component of team participation. It is the same concept that sports teams rely on to achieve success. Group-powered commitment provides support to others honoring the goals of the team and disciplinary consequences for those who waver. It is one of the strongest elements holding a team together.

In sports, as more members of the team buy into team goals, the greater the effort that is put forth in pursuit of those goals. This is how greater chances for success are made possible.

In war, this concept also holds true. In the words of General George S. Patton, Jr., "Magnificent! Compared to war all other forms of human endeavor shrink to insignificance." He also said, "The most important thing in any organization is the creation of a soul, which is based on pride in the unit."

In Vietnam, my men fought as I commanded them to because they understood the power of my commitment to the group and because of their commitment to one another as 'brothers.' They worked for the team goals effortlessly and without hesitation.

7th Benefit: Expanded Problem Identification & Resolution

We stopped on a trail in Vietnam to take a break. I sat next to my squad leader and looking down spied a small, red, black and yellow snake. My understanding was that coral snakes were not indigenous to Vietnam and was concerned.

"What kind of snake is that?" I asked.

My squad leader glanced over, swiftly grabbed his machete, and in the blink of an eye, sliced it to pieces. He smiled. "I reckon we don'ts got to worry about it." To this day, this stands as one brief example of expanded problem identification and resolution in action. In short, the positive value each individual can contribute is an asset that supports the virtues of group-powered commitment.

8th Benefit: Competitiveness as a Positive Driver

Individual competitiveness appears to be a natural part of being human. We all like to win. It is possible however for competitiveness in a team to enhance productivity and expand upon the team's goals.

To encourage joint problem solving and a utilization of a team's diverse assets, a team leader needs to define the winning terms for the team as a whole and not just the individual. Further, for this approach to be successful, the team's assets including the diversity in perspectives, ideas and problem-solving abilities must be taken into consideration. These are in effect tools by which the team can best achieve their shared goals and objectives.

The development of the nuclear bomb was brought forward under the pressures of an ongoing World War by teams of scientists who were competing in a race. Despite arguments and disagreements over problem assessments and resolutions two viable, operational designs were produced.

As destructive as nuclear weapons are, the scientific advantages of this work had a major impact on the creation of the world we now live in. It also brought World War II to an end earlier than would have been possible otherwise. Ultimately it was a team who won that battle. Which is to say, being on the same team is the only way 'we' can win the battle of survival.

THE INHERENT PROBLEMS OF TEAMS

"Coming together is a beginning,
Staying together is progress,
And working together is success."

— Henry Ford

Internal Problems Inherent to Teams

STRUCTURE	LEADERSHIP	BELIEF
• Bureaucracy by its nature advances 'order' over goals and accomplishments. While not bad per se, this inevitably hinders goals achievement. • Structure requires defined rules and regulations. • Must have balance and equitable ability to perform varied, sometimes opposing functions effectively.	• Personal advancement over achieving team goals is the most frequent problem at all levels of leadership. An alternate vision of what the actual goal is or should be, often creates misalignment as to the best direction to pursue and achieve goals. • Provide direction and guidance in approach and monitor progress. Adjust as necessary. • Oversee team growth and change.	• Belief is always presented as fact. If we do A, then B shall follow. Belief wavers if the result is not apparent or does not seem reachable. External beliefs can impact and overtake a team, changing its actions while maintaining and even strengthening the original goals. • Establish and maintain belief in team goals to ensure commitment. • Monitor belief to forestall diversion from intended goal.

Addressing Internal Problems Thru Realignment

STRUCTURE	LEADERSHIP	BELIEF
These may range from relatively mild and easy changes to rules and regulations that completely restructure team relationships and redefine the purpose of different team components.	The job of leadership is to identify what needs to be done to achieve team goals and take appropriate action to ensure it gets done. There are innumerable options to accomplish any given team goal, from minor adjustments to significant changes in direction or new leadership.	Most beliefs are founded on faith more than on fact. This works well for teams because faith defies change brought about by an evolving discovery of facts. If factual evidence is not a requirement, then altering the meaning of faith is easy.

THE DETRIMENTAL HANDICAPS OF A TEAM

"Lack of loyalty is one of the major causes of failure in every walk of life."

— Napoleon Hill

Throughout human history, from the very beginning down to the present moment, holding power has been an innate concern of every member of a team. And despite wanting control over our own lives, most of us are willing to buy into becoming part of a team because it is embedded in our DNA that this is how we succeed as a species. While we want to retain control for ourselves, once we become part of a team. We take pride in it. We hold strong beliefs and are uplifted when we feel we are a part of something greater than ourselves. We're willing to sacrifice, even give our life, for the success of our team. We surrender to power and require others to do the same. At a national level this is called patriotism.

As American citizens, we commit to believing we live in the greatest country. We believe this despite any evidence to the contrary to dispute it, sometimes violently, with those who do not share our commitment as we think they ought to.

1st Detrimental Handicap: Hierarchy & Leadership

Leaders are required to maintain certain levels in the hierarchy and over time, this becomes more powerful than leadership. A brief review of history demonstrates the problem inherent in attempting to balance the collision between power and a concern for the individual.

We form teams with goals of self-preservation and prosperity and as we succeed we want more and become reluctant to share what is gained with others. Teams grow from families, to tribes, to kingdoms, and finally to empires.

Every empire follows the same course.
A struggle to rise.
The consolidation of power.
The constraints to exercise power and rule.
The empire's decline.
Death of the empire.

One of the first historically recognized empires was that of the Akkadians. Their ruler, Sargon the Great, established the first recognized dynasty in the world. Dynasty requires extreme nepotism amid the belief that god is on your side.

Sargon's son Rimbush succeeded him, followed by his brother Manistushu, who may have hastened his brother's departure. Finally, Sargon's grandson Naram-Sin ruled. This first dynasty was the shortest on record and served as the prototype of empires rising, conquering, ruling and then declining. Every great empire has followed on this path.

Alexander the Great conquered a vast territory beyond what any other leader had accomplished. When he died his empire declined and disintegrated. By contrast, Greece opted for democracy and not a dynasty. They left us some of mankind's greatest achievements but their empire crumbled.

Rome created an empire that would last four centuries and leave a lasting impact down to this very day, but it too eventually fell apart. The Egyptians built an empire that lasted for thousands of years but ultimately did not survive.

In Asia, Qin Shi Huangdi conquered all of the neighboring kingdoms and formed an empire that encompassed most of modern China. He is credited with beginning construction on the Great Wall of China and yet his empire collapsed. What followed were numerous dynasties who made their own tremendous contributions to the history of empires but they too could not escape the path to final fragmentation.

Temujin Borjigin led the Mongols to conquer the greatest amount of territory ever. The Great Wall of China did not stop him. He rode around it, and ultimately included China in his empire which was ruled for a long time by his son. He became known as Genghis Khan and was such an inspiring leader his armies won battles screaming his name long after his death. His empire, however mighty, also ended in demise.

Every empire we have ever seen has fallen in large part due to the problems inherent in the dynamics of a team. Beginning with the conflict between, the concern of the individual, and concern for the team. The result of this conflict is a struggle for the balance of power.

2nd Handicap: Prioritizing A Win At All Costs

When we prioritize winning at all costs, often we negate the team's goals. The intrinsic struggle for power within a team breeds competitiveness amongst its members and brings about the question of who is better suited to be the leader?

This competition when it works, can aid in defining who is better suited for team leadership. More often, what tends to happen is we create a battle for who will win the role of leadership and it becomes of paramount importance when compared to the team's goals. This is true even when the opponents believe they are all best suited to lead the team.

The problem is, given the belief that the team must reach its goals at all costs, the competition for leadership becomes an at-all-costs proposition as well. Therefore, individual advancement and power are implicit in this equation and actively work against the shared commitment to win as a team, and not just as an individual.

Consider this. In every competition you enter, you first work to prepare yourself to be as capable to compete within the set rules as possible. This is true whether the competition is physical, intellectual or social. Second, you search for an edge suited to your abilities and accomplishments at that stage. Third, you consider and may follow a course that pushes the boundaries of the rules, or you may completely disregard the set boundaries. If winning at all costs is the mission the blending of boundaries becomes a plausible alternative.

3rd Handicap: Focus on Destroying Opposition vs. Goal Attainment

Problem resolution from this perspective is destructive and counterproductive. This is the way wars begin. Whether you want to attain the next phase of power for the good of accomplishing the team's goals, for individual advancement, or both, the overwhelming drive is to gain the position to hold the power. All other concerns become subordinate to achieving the desired position of power. The problem becomes not 'how do we defeat that other man's army?' But rather, 'how do I get him out of my way so I can have his position of power?'

When the drive is to move upward in power it becomes more difficult to follow and support the leader you believe you should replace because following him and supporting him then seems detrimental not only to the team's goals but to your goals. This position leads to falsely defining the problems that are preventing you from holding the power you want to attain.

4th Handicap: Formed Factions Challenge Group Loyalty

When group commitment fractures into factions loyalty to the team becomes compromised. This is at the heart of team destruction and is native to the entire concept of working within a team. A loss of focus on a team's goals for whatever reason, including a shift in alliances and loyalty plants the seed for a team's failure. This is true whether the team is little league baseball or your nation.

The development of small sub-groups is integral to the way in which teams operate. These sub-groups when they work in concert with the team's goals represent that belief that all participating are doing the right thing and will therefore reap a share of the coming prosperity.

In practice, we preach and honor team commitment as we must, but we do not nurture it as we should. Instead we depend on slogans, be the "Wildcats rule!" Or "Make America Great Again!" These are useless instruments meant to coerce support without true commitment and are more useful in motivating us to chase power than to accomplish our unified goals.

5th Handicap: Divided Loyalties Limit Individual Contributions

When a division of loyalty occurs within a team, it inevitably limits the contributions an individual member can make. For example, if your goal is to seek power there are numerous ways in which to choose not to contribute and thereby sabotage the leader you wish to replace.

You can present information in a format that is not very useful. You can overstate or understate information so that it bends decisions in the wrong direction. You can prevent subordinates from bringing information forward or see that said contributions are poorly received. Or you can simply fail to show up or prevent others from doing so. The permutations of this handicap are both subtle and varied.

6th Handicap: Diminishing Prosperity

Team prosperity diminishes for two major reasons. First, the team is less successful overall. Remember Woolworth's, Montgomery Ward, Packard, Blockbuster? Second, one of the major attractions of power is a greater share in the prosperity gained by the team's contributions.

According to a report from the Economic Policy Institute, the average CEO pay is 271 times the nearly $58,000 average annual pay of the typical American worker. Compare this to 1978, when CEO earnings were roughly 30 times the typical worker's salary.

Walmart paid its median worker $19,177 last year while Chief Executive Doug McMillon earned $22.8 million, according to a security filings. (Wall Street Journal. April 20, 2018) This is 1,188 times the median worker's earnings.

Forget all of our other problems. This type of continuing and growing pay gap, which is neither unique or unusual, is likely, in and of itself, to destroy the United States. As I write this, the president has canceled pay increases for all federal employees. This is shortly after granting a trillion-dollar tax cut to billionaires.

7th Handicap: Analysis Becomes a Weapon of Internecine Warfare

Mark Twain had it right when he said, "There are lies, damned lies, and statistics." In my role as a city manager, I presented three categories of data and information to my councils.

1. Information that was certified accurate per an accepted, identified source or sources.
2. Information that was likely accurate per the identified data and information sources available.
3. Information that was my best guess.

Regardless of the category of information, it may or may not have been correct and yet, acceptable and 'effective decision-making' was the expected result.

In internecine power wars, analysis can become a weapon when the information it is based on is certified to be absolutely true and therefore irrefutable. In the most severe cases, it is simply called lying.

Accepting any analysis as absolute is a surefire way to take another step onto a minefield and get blown up! It is the job of leaders to use analysis as a reliable supplement to effective decision making. It is a mistake to utilize it as the only deciding factor.

8th Handicap: Support Based on Self Loyalty and Not Team Goals

A leader who is more concerned about loyalty to himself than the talent and skills of his subordinates isn't leading to accomplish the team's goals. Rather, he is concerned with his own power and how to best maintain it.

A man whose goal it is to gain more power will be most concerned with attaining loyal support for himself. He will not trust or enable anyone who is more committed to the team than they are to him. He will use loyalty to impact decisions in a manner he perceives will benefit him and not the team.

The board of directors of many major corporations participate in a long, drawn-out process, and often a power struggle, over the replacement of their CEO because the organization is fixated on loyalty rather than the ability to accomplished team goals. This happens in part because very few CEOs train their successors. They fear being replaced sooner than later if a viable replacement is so readily available.

PART 3

PROPOSED AMENDMENTS TO THE CONSTITUTION

THE IMMUTABLE LAWS OF HUMAN ORGANIZATION

"Each House may determine the Rules of its Proceedings..."

— The Constitution of the United States, Article 1, Section 5, Paragraph 2

The Law of Human Organizations is not pretty good. It is not mostly accurate. It is not a nice guideline. It is immutable. Alternative words for immutable include: unchallengeable, absolute, unavailable, incontrovertible, indisputable, undeniable and not able to be forfeited.

All human organizations, no matter the reason for which they are formed, or how they are structured and managed to achieve their goals, will deteriorate over time into a mechanism for some people to tell other people what to do. This leads to a diversion from the operation of the organization to a focus on personal goals and the attainment of personal power.

1st Corollary to the Immutable Laws of Human Organizations

The first corollary is the only outcome there can be. The only factors affecting the first corollary are: time, opportunity and vaccinations.

When the issue becomes attaining and maintaining power, corruption will always ensue, and it may take many forms because humans have the capacity to behave in devious ways.

The Immutable Law of Human Organizations requires us to take action to alter the structure of our government, in order to create viable mechanisms that will allow us to effectively deal with modern-world problems. To be clear, we cannot fix anything by protesting, or filing lawsuits, or by electing good people. While we should do all of those things, these are not actions which will allow us to supplant the structure of power the oligarchy has created.

What we're facing is a modern-day Gordian Knot. We must first separate the pillars before we can begin to correct the problems.

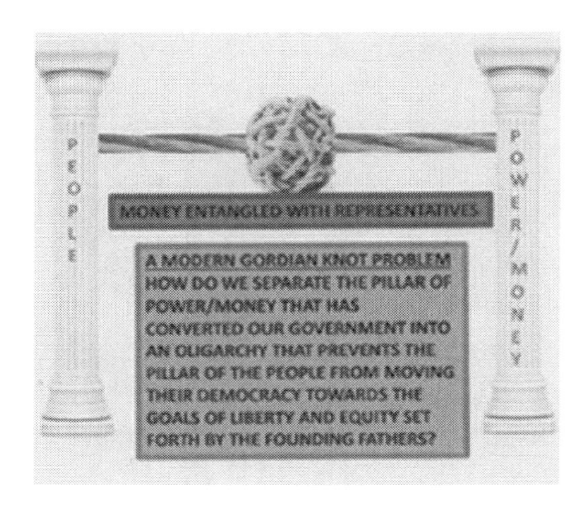

There are two ways to cut the Gordian knot and begin to resolve the current troubles of the United States. First, there is the bloody way. That is, we have a civil war or a bloody revolution, and people get killed. When you consider the increase in mass shootings, and the recent idiocies, such as attempting to pass laws that protect people who drive into protestors, it seems evident that we are already on a bloody path.

The second way, as proposed by our founding father in the Constitution, is a method of peaceful sedition and a bloodless revolution. In other words, an amendment to the Constitution.

Those boys may not have known all they were doing in 1787, but they knew they could not predict the future and handle all of our problems for us. So they gave us a mechanism to make changes in a peaceful way, with the full expectation that we would do just that. I think their confidence in us was overabundant, but we shall see.

The challenge is that Constitutional amendments are incredibly difficult to achieve. The Constitution of the United States was adapted in large part because the Bill of Rights presented the first ten agreed upon Amendments. In the two-hundred-and-thirty years since, 11,000 amendments have been proposed and we have passed seventeen amendments or about one every thirteen or fourteen years. One amendment which has yet to be introduced is one which could significantly alter our government's operations.

We must remember that the idea of creating a government "of the people, by the people, and for the people," was an outrageous one. It had never been done before, and is akin to building a faster-than-light engine. It may result in the velocity you desire but there is no way to predict how it will function and what course it might take.

The idea of checks and balances proposed by our founding fathers was a good one, but it only addressed the operators and not the engine. With operators inevitably moving in pursuit of their own prosperity, seeking power, screwing up our engine and ultimately selling out we are bound to reach the level of inequity we are experiencing today. What we have then, beyond the challenge of fixing the engine is the resistance by those in power who are benefitting greatly from the inequity we need to remedy.

The good news is resistance simply means the challenge will be a difficult one. In reviewing the history of *Home sapiens* on this planet, when it comes to human organizations, there are two patterns that constantly repeat that drive the rise and fall of said constructs.

The first is the need to consolidate power if the rise is to be successful, which always leads to the grabbing of power for personal use and veering off of the intended path for the organization. The second pattern is devious and hard to see. It is the impact of power from outside of the organization which bends it toward alternate goals. External power usually operates within the realm of financial corruption via bribery that is either direct or behind-the-scenes.

So, are power and money the problem?

No. They are the mechanism. Greed and stupidity are the problems, just as they have been since we walked off the African Savannah.

2nd Corollary to the Immutable Laws of Human Organizations

There is no cure for the 1st Corollary. There is however, a vaccine which entails a regular review of the way things are going and to make changes to the operational parameters of the organization with the goal to achieve course corrections and to limit the abuse of power without gumming up the works.

In simple terms and to understand what needs to be worked back into the engine that can place the country back on track to how it was intended to run we need to consider for a moment the Second Corollary.

There is no permanent fix to the engine. We need to do our best to get it running in a way that the operators will have difficulty meddling with, and then pay attention when the emergency lights on the dash advise us it is due for another tune up. However, the idea is to fix the engine not necessarily to change the people running the operation.

The power of Congress to set its own rules is laid out in the Constitution of the United States, Article 1, Section 5, Paragraph 2: "Each House may determine the Rules of its Proceedings..." The problem inherent in this is that they make the rules, so they can break the rules, and there are no controlling factors such as discussion and seeking majority approval to limit or slow the changes they choose to make. We need to set rules that will ensure Congress does their job and operates the engine in a reasonable manner.

THE MAKINGS OF A CIVIL WAR

"Civil War? What does that mean?
Is there any foreign war?
Isn't every war fought between men, between brothers?"

— Victor Hugo

The Republic of the United States has long been a world empire in terms of its power and influence. Its many accomplishment have led humanity toward a better, more prosperous future. It has also acted in ways that worked against its promise of a government by the consent of the governed and its commitment to ensuring the individual rights of life, liberty and the pursuit of happiness.

Instead of our full support to these promises we have paid lip service and that has allowed those in power to enhance their control and increase their own power. We're facing tremendous earnings inequity. In 2016, the top 1% controlled a record high 38.6% of the country's wealth. The bottom 90% controlled 22.8%, down from nearly a third in 1989. Some CEOs earn in excess of $9,000 per hour, and we cannot get minimum wage to $15 per hour, which if it kept the pace with inflation would be around $22 per hour.

In actuality, the healthcare system in the United States is operated as a for-profit business without any real concern for people's health. As such, any equity of care is impossible to achieve.

"We have gender inequality with women still struggling against a glass ceiling in the economy and an idiot ceiling in society with a strong rape culture. When you go further into gender and discuss issues such as homosexuality and transgender any kind of equity is vociferously challenged."

"There is of course, race inequity with black unemployment twice that of white and a major, open demonstrating of white supremacy groups, who have significant support at the highest levels and who consider all minorities to be at best second class citizens and probably no citizens at all."

"Access to medical care is so unbalanced, there was a recent case of a man winning a $1,000,000 lottery and immediately getting a doctor's appointment, which he hadn't been able to afford for some time, and discovering he had stage 4 cancer. He died 23 days later. That is only illustrative of the inequity of a healthcare system based on profit. This grows worse as those controlling the government aggressively attempt to eliminate the Affordable Care Act, largely, in the opinion of some, because it was created under a black president's leadership, while refusing to even address the many health issues we have in our country."

"There is the gross inequity of spending six-hundred-and-eleven billion dollars on our military, while China, Russia, Saudi Arabia, India, France, the United Kingdom, Japan and Germany spend a combined five-hundred-and-ninety billion. And we're not any safer for it."

— Stockholm International Peace Research Institute, 2017

This is happening while many of our soldier's families need access to welfare assistance to survive. There is massive excess in spending as evidence by programs such as the $100 billion development of Lockheed's F-35 Strike Force Jet Fighter. Despite the program failing to meet requirements, an additional $100 billion have been allocated to it. To make matters worse, these inequities and many others are being completely ignored by our government. In the first year of the current administration one major bill was passed and proposed as a tax reform, when in effect, was little more than a gift to the wealthiest 1% who own a majority of our country and have beyond significant wealth our lawmakers in their pockets. The way the passing of the bill was conducted, without hearings, limited discussion and by bending the rules further supports that we are indeed in a fragile state.

As a result, there is much discontent in this country, and it is beginning to give way to the sort of violence and deaths that preceded the Civil War.

Mass killings in the United States since 2000, in which the dead numbered in double figures:

March 21, 2005	Red Lake, MN	10 dead
April 3, 2009	Binghamton, NY	14 dead
November 5, 2009	Fort Hood, TX	13 dead
December 14, 2012	Sandy Hook Elementary School — Newton, CT	26 dead (20 children)
December 2015	San Bernardino, CA	14 dead
June 12, 2016	Pulse Night Club — Orlando, FL	49 dead
April 16, 2017	Virginia Tech University — Blacksburg, VA	32 dead
October 1, 2017	Las Vegas, NV	58 dead (+ 422 wounded)
November 5, 2017	Sutherland, TX	25 dead
February 15, 2018	Parkland, FL	17 dead
May 19, 2018	San Antonio, TX	10 dead

Massive protests, including the ramming of a car into groups of protestors have led to the introduction of legislation that exempts drivers from liability for hitting anyone protesting in a public right-of-way. This legislation is supported in some states.

In the media, there is an outpouring of vitriol which includes a straightforward advocacy for killing those of whom we do not approve. We refuse to a hold police officer accountable for shooting and killing a twelve-year-old boy with a toy gun within three-seconds of encountering him. Then we rage about prosecution of a black man who kneels in protest of that and similar acts during the national anthem at a football game. We justify and celebrate his being held accountable and losing his job.

One man kills a child without justification, and we do not hold him responsible. Another man protests. He hurts no-one. He kills no-one and we are outraged.

A civil war is approaching. It will not be fought on separate sides of a geographic line. It will be fought over whether we support the ideals of our nation as expressed by our founding fathers. Or whether we believe others are inferior to us and therefore we should get what we can take and they should get what they deserve.

In essence, we have become an oligarchy. The wealthy control our elections, and our government. They command most of the media and are skilled at waving 'fake news' as a cape in our faces. Like the bull chases the red cape, we chase the immigrant, the Mexican, the black, the woman, the LGBQT community, the 'libtard,' the snowflake, and any other label we can think of, but never see who wields the cape. It appears to be enough for us to identify a target for our anger and our fear so that we may exercise our rage, and like lemmings, rush over the cliff to meet our end. All the while, we ignore the oligarchy that is creating problems through its misuse of power.

Before you become upset with what I am stating, and it prevents you from rational analysis and logical action, consider this: As set forth previously throughout this book, what is happening now, is not new. It stems from a simple problem inherent in all human organizations. It is a condition we cannot avoid or cure. However, we can manage it, and in so doing we could deal with our problems honestly and perhaps survive as a species in the long run.

THE PEACEFUL SEDITION

"The Bill of Rights is a born rebel.
It reeks with sedition. In every clause it shakes its fist
In the face of constituted authority...it is the one
Guarantee of human freedom to the American people."

— LaFollette's Magazine, January 1920

As children we are conditioned to believe in fables, myths and other non-factual stories to hold some real meaning for us. In mythology for example, the legends of twelve, fantastic labors turn the Greek demigod Heracles, the son of Zeus and Alcmene, into Hercules. In the adult mind, while no real belief in his existence remains, we hold onto a lingering concept. Think for a moment how our vocabulary includes the terms Herculean task or Herculean effort. Terms by the way, which seem to be express exactly what lies ahead of us as we attempt to fix the engine of this country.

Consider the birth of Rome which is based on the story of Romulus and Remus, orphans raised by wolves. In a fight for dominance, Romulus wins and creates Rome. There is no factual basis to this, but since Rome exists there must somehow be some shade of truth in the story.

And what about God? Much of the human race holds a belief that there is a God, but the concept of god began as a way to explain the natural world around us. Hence, we created the god of lightning and thunder, of volcanoes and earthquakes and of any number of, at the time, incomprehensible occurrences. Before I continue, please understand I do not dispute others' beliefs or seek to undermine them. In fact, the phrase "pursuit of Happiness" used by our founding fathers had two basic intentions. The first was concerning property rights. They did not like the king taking their land whenever he felt like it. The second, was the responsibility of any educated individual to evaluate the universe and find an accommodation for what he discovers, and how he reacts to others' beliefs.

They did not believe in a government-dictated system of religion and wanted to protect an individual's right to pursue the questions. Yet religions today are a major element in how we form beliefs, despite their basis on non-factual stories that encourage action and force others to abide those formed beliefs. These stories, even if untrue, resonate with humans because we have an inner need to find someone or something outside of ourselves whom we believe holds control and offers protection.

The Role of Fake News

Today's stories come to us in the form of fake news. In times past with limited communication, the use of fake news had its limits but this didn't prevent it from starting wars. Now, we have worldwide media serving up an overabundance of information that is accessible to virtually anyone. The challenge has become how to distinguish real news from fake news. Headlines are crafted to sound alarms: 'War with Korea,' 'CIA is incompetent,' FBI is biased,' and the list goes on, but there is more damage being done.

Consider the divisiveness of criticizing large portions of the population, and the constant slurs and outrageous slander of women, and all the 'truly good people' in the white supremacist movement. We have labeled Mexican rapists. Continued some form of prejudice against blacks. Insulted the military by insulting 'Gold Star parents' and kneeling during the national anthem. All of our rage and protest is laid bare on Facebook posts and Twitter comments and yet our outrage and resistance to this behavior is akin to a bull chasing a red cape.

What we are expressing via these newly created channels of global communication may not mean anything and may in fact get us killed or enslaved. Everybody can point out what they think should be changed. Some of us may be right, and some of us may be wrong. What no-one is talking about is what it will take to make the changes we do need to implement. Most of us believe this is simply a matter of electing the 'right' people.

The simple truth however, is that no matter who we elect, they will not be able to implement the necessary changes. The structure of government will not allow for this to happen and that is what must change and only 'we' can change it. While there are numerous changes needed to address the damage already done, to change this nation, we must change The Constitution. We must alter the engine to accomplish three outcomes, which are required to positively affect the operation of the organization that is our government.

3 Outcomes We Must Pursue

1. We must significantly reduce the impact of private money on our elections and on the operation of government.

2. We must require a complete, open accounting of those who desire election. This includes an accounting of their finances and all aspects of their personal and professional life.

3. We must remove the power of Congress to set their own rules and set the rules for them, and we must more clearly define the powers and limitations of the Executive and Judicial branches.

What follows are the proposals I believe can help us achieve these outcomes. The challenge of actually amending The Constitution I must leave to 'we the people.' And please note, the required amendments to alter the structure and operation of our government must contain all of the following elements. Implementing only bits and pieces will not help us succeed with this mission and will be time and effort wasted. But before we consider the amendments, it's important to understand the role of sedition in all of this.

Why peaceful sedition?

The amendments proposed in this book could result in integral changes to how we govern ourselves. And they could be considered sedition. We cannot accomplish all of the necessary amendments by thinking we can simply elect good people and support good ideas and everything will work out. The Immutable Law of Human Organizations will not allow it. The organization is too weighed down by structures aimed at attaining and retaining power and it is too susceptible to corruption.

The United States has become an oligarchy, run by wealthy individuals and corporations. It will continue on that path until the people change it. Resistance from senators and congressman has kept them from total control, but the despot who Gouverneur Morris warned us about in 1787 is sitting in the White House attempting to implement a dictatorship.

The options available to us are either a Civil War, or what was given to us with the expectation we would nurture it with intelligence and wisdom. We can amend The Constitution. We can exercise peaceful sedition as our founding fathers intended for us to.

Why should we focus on making the amendments I will bring forth in the pages that follow? The answer is that with so many issues, including climate control, gun control, and sensible immigration laws, we need to focus on addressing the issues that will most quickly get our government back on track to operating as a government that is governing by the consent of its people.

I do not suggest that every element will be covered or addressed in the best possible way. I am attempting to engage my fellow Americans by helping them to realize what we need to put a stop to and what we need to reignite into action. If we continue to allow lawmakers to play power games and changing the rules at will, as a nation we will accomplish nothing, and our country will meet its end.

AMENDMENTS TO THE CONSTITUTION TO RESTRUCTURE GOVERNMENT

"Any constitutional amendment that simply gives Congress the option of regulating campaign finance fails to immediately achieve what the American people want, and that is a complete reversal of Citizens United and other Supreme Court decisions that have allowed corporations and the wealthy few to drown out the voices of everyday voters."

— Ted Deutch

The Role of Financing in Elections

Section 1: Proposals to achieve intended outcomes

Sections 1.1 through 1.2 deal with issues of money impacting elections before and after the fact, lobbying, limiting the right to vote, gerrymandering, sufficient voting sites, setting regular voting with extended time periods, preventing game-playing with interim appointments, and eliminating the Electoral College.

1.1 All contributions to candidates, parties, or in support of a given issue shall include a clear identification of the individual(s) making the donation. All business and other organizations shall indicate the individual(s) who decided upon the contribution. PACs will no longer be allowed to donate or spend money on behalf of an individual. They may support a given issue but not in a manner that demonstrates intent to support an individual.

1.2 The maximum contribution by any individual during a given election period (one year) shall be a total of $100,000. The maximum contribution by a corporation during a given election period (one year) shall be $100,000 with the individual authorizing the donation identified.

1.3 Contributions made on behalf of others must include written documentation of the consent of the individual(s) for whom the donation is provided and of said individual(s) being eligible voters.

1.4 Churches and non-profit organizations are prohibited from donating to political campaigns, including the funding of political advertisements.

1.5 Funds raised for a campaign for election shall not be used for other purposes. To do so shall be a felony violation of the federal law. Campaign chests of retiring or defeated members will not be converted to a cash retirement fund for them.

1.6 For federal elections, any citizen shall be eligible to vote, unless disqualified due to a legal action such as a conviction of violating federal law.

1.7 Identification for any voter shall be by fingerprint or retinal scan when such technology is available. Post-election, a review of the IDs shall be conducted to ensure that no individual has attempted to cast a vote more than once or to vote illegally. No other ID shall be required. Interference with the casting of a vote shall not be allowed. Authorities may question the validity of a vote, and federal authorities shall review such allegations and determine if a vote will be allowed.

1.8 A bipartisan federal commission will determine the boundaries of all districts to avoid gerrymandering or other attempts to interfere with fair voting.

1.9 A bipartisan federal commission will review all voting sites and require the opening of additional sites if determined necessary to allow equity in the ability to cast a vote.

1.10 Regular federal elections will be held in even-numbered years. Voting will begin on the first Tuesday in November and shall continue through the following Sunday. Special elections will be held within ninety days of a vacancy occurring if the vacancy leaves open a period of 120 or more days. Special elections will be held on a Friday through Sunday. If there are fewer than 120 days left in the vacancy, the governor of said state may appoint a replacement or choose to leave it vacant.

1.11 The Electoral College shall be eliminated and individual votes shall determine the winner in all elections.

1.12 No individual who has served in the Congress of the United States, after completing his tenure, shall be allowed to be employed as a lobbyist or act in the capacity of a lobbyist for the rest of his or her life.

States shall set their own rules for elections to office in their state, so long as they do not interfere with federal elections.

Candidate Transparency

Section 2: Proposals to achieve intended outcomes

Sections 2.1 through 2.5 deal with setting minimal requirements for transparency for all candidates, and includes financial, physical health, accuracy of military service, and a formal policy on review sessions that are televised and networked for all to observe and not run by politicians.

2.1 Any individual choosing to run for election to a federal office shall undergo a complete transparency review of all financial and business dealings. This shall include: the release of income tax filings for the previous ten (10) years; the complete holdings of wealth and property, including any not held in the United States and any held by immediate family members; any outstanding debt owed personally or in a business capacity, including the amount and to whom it is owed; any legal actions personally or in a business capacity whether ongoing or completed in the previous (10) years; and all connections to any individual or business that might involve a legal obligation, including identifying any settlements to any individual or business that includes a privacy clause. Said review shall be public.

2.2 Any individual choosing to run for office will be required to undergo a physical examination by a federally appointed physician. The results of the exam will be made public. No result will be disqualifying.

2.3 Any individual choosing to run for election shall provide verification of any claimed qualifications of military service, educational accomplishment, and technical certification.

2.4 Items 2.1, 2.2, and 2.3 will be completed and released by March 31 of the election year. The country will be geographically divided into six primary districts. On the first and third Saturday in April, May and June of that year, a primary election will be held for each party, consecutively in the primary districts.

In the second week of August, September, and October, the TV networks and any other service providers will contribute to public service by paying for the broadcast of three policy review sessions with the presidential candidates. The hosts will be chosen and questions will be prepared and asked by a bipartisan commission and cover the issues as follows: August—the economy, September—national defense and diplomatic relations, October—all other issues as determined by the commission.

All candidates will be real-time fact checked. All candidates will be interrupted and requested to answer the question if the host feels they are wandering off topic. This will be done twice for any given topic. A third such interruption will result in a ruling of question unanswered and the next question will posed.

The vice-presidential candidates will have one policy review session between the September and October sessions of the presidential candidates. The commission will determine appropriate questioning.

The Power of Congress

Section 3: Proposals to achieve intended outcomes

Sections 3.1 through 3.11 will define certain rules of operation for Congress starting with the elimination of the power to set their own rules.

3.1 The power of Congress to set its own rules as noted in the Constitution of the United States, Article 1, Section 5, Paragraph 2, "Each House may determine the Rules of its Proceedings..." shall be removed. The authority to punish its members for disorderly conduct with the concurrence of 2/3 of the members and expel a member shall not be deleted. The following section shall set forth the required actions and rules for both the Senate and the House of Representatives:

3.2 At the beginning of each term, the day after swearing in, the Senate and the House of Representatives shall meet and take the following actions:

(1) appoint all committee members

(2) set the work schedule for the year, with a minimum of two thousand hours scheduled

(3) set a schedule to have a budget prepared for consideration for adoption by the first work day of August. If that deadline is not met, the members of both the Senate and the House shall be required to be at their seats in their respective chambers for ten hours a day, six days a week until the budget is ready to be considered for adoption.

From the beginning of this period until such time as the budget is adopted, no member shall be provided any form of payment or benefits. If the budget is not adopted by October 1 of the budget year, the members of both the Senate and the House of Representatives shall be required to be at their seats in their respective chambers for twelve hours a day for seven days a week until it has been adopted. From October 1 of the budget year until the budget is adopted, no member of shall receive any pay or benefits

(4) set a schedule for consideration of other legislation by allowing thirty-days for each member to set forth legislation they wish to be considered. All such legislation will be reviewed to require members with the same concerns to consider consolidating their requests. No request shall include unrelated topics. No limit shall be set on the number of requests made. All requests shall be scheduled for review by the appropriate committees.

3.3 Every member shall be at his appropriate workstation, i.e. Senate or House Chambers, Committee, or office, during the scheduled hours of work. A member may have an excused absence for a death in his/her immediate family, or a documented and critical medical emergency. A non-excused absence shall require disciplinary action as follows:

First offense requires a disciplinary letter noting the failure to be at the required work station performing the required work activity. The letter will be placed in a file open to public access.

Second offense and subsequent offenses require a disciplinary letter to be placed in the file and a loss of pay for the time in question.

Five disciplinary offenses will require the House in question to vote on whether the member in question should be expelled. If the member is not expelled, an additional five offenses will require automatic expulsion.

3.4 Committee appointments of Chairperson will be made by the majority party. The minority party will appoint a senior member who will act as Assistant Chairperson. The Chairperson will set all meetings in cooperation with the Assistant Chairperson, including ensuring sufficient prior notice to all members that they may reasonably make accommodations to attend. Both the Chairperson and the Assistant Chairperson will determine who shall be called as witnesses on any given legislation. All witnesses shall be given a reasonable opportunity to present their testimony.

The purpose of committee hearings is to hear and gain information regarding potential legislation. It shall not be the purpose of committee hearings to investigate members of the Executive, Judiciary, or Legislative branches of government.

Such investigations shall be accomplished under a separate section of this amendment.

No member(s) of Congress, individually or in a group, shall accept paid travel, lodging, food, gifts, and/or entertainment expenses from any individual or corporation to gain information regarding any legislation or potential legislation without prior approval from the majority and minority party leaders in both Houses. Any such approved trip shall produce a report from each individual to ensure that any gift or entertainment had a value of less than $100. If the value was in excess of that amount, the individual in question must remit the amount over $100 to the federal treasury.

3.5 Votes in committee on any given piece of legislation shall be advisory to the respective House. All legislation proposed shall be published for one week prior to its consideration by the full body. During that period:

- any member may propose an amendment to the proposed legislation.

- no item unrelated to the legislation may be attached to the legislation as an amendment or by any other process.

- if an amendment is contested by the author of the legislation as not being related, it

- shall be held and treated as a separate piece of legislation.

- a vote on the proposed amendments and the proposed legislation shall be conducted with a twenty-four-hour notice on the time of the vote. If ten members protest that the time allowed for review is inadequate, the vote shall be delayed for seven days.

- Amendments in the order received shall receive an up or down vote to amend the proposed legislation. The proposed legislation shall then receive an up or down vote, by which it shall be passed or rejected.

- any attempt to modify the language of the amendments or the proposed language prior to or after the vote shall be a felony and shall be prosecuted as such. If convicted of such a felony, the individual in question will be expelled from Congress and may never serve in that capacity again, in addition to, any penalties for the conviction of the felony.

3.6 All voting on the passage of legislation shall be by roll-call. All members are required to cast a vote. No filibuster shall be allowed, although members may receive an extended period to debate the vote. Members must stay on topic if the extension of time is granted for debate. The legislation and the roll-call vote shall be published on a website available to the public.

3.7 The right of pre-implementation appeal may be exercised by any combination of senators and representatives equaling ten percent of the total of both Houses. Such appeal shall go immediately to the Supreme Court, which shall take immediate action to review and determine the constitutionality of any legislation before it is put into effect. If necessary, the Court will immediately return to session to do this if it is not currently in session.

3.8 Robert's Rules of Order shall be the controlling document for the debate and voting process on both committee work, and for the body as a whole. In no case shall rules be utilized to limit debate, or to delay or forestall a vote on proposed legislation. Votes shall be scheduled with adequate notice and held when they are scheduled.

3.9 The Senate shall vote for approval for any nominee of the president to the Supreme Court with a required threshold of sixty votes needed for said approval. Upon receiving a nomination for the Supreme Court from any sitting president at any point in his term, the review and vote shall take place within ninety-days of receipt of the nomination.

3.10 Congress shall not be exempt from any laws passed by previous sessions of Congress and shall not exempt itself from any laws it passes now or in the future. Members of Congress shall participate in contributing to Social Security and shall have no other retirement set aside for them. Previous awards of retirement shall cease immediately upon the adoption of this amendment, and any funds set aside for payment of said retirement shall be transferred to the Social Security Fund. Retirees can receive Social Security disbursements on the same basis as everyone else.

3.11 Senators and representatives shall receive an annual raise equivalent in dollar value, not percentage, to the amount of the average increase for Social Security recipients. No additional remuneration shall be received unless approved by the electorate.

The Powers of the President

Section 4: Proposals to achieve intended outcomes

Sections 4.1 through 4.4 will clarify some of the powers of the president, including the use of military force, issuing of executive orders, clarifying some of the causes which may result in impeachment, and limiting the power of presidential pardon.

4.1 The President of the United States as Commander in Chief may dispatch military forces to any place in the world where the president believes it is necessary for national defense. If those forces engage in any combat action on the ground, in the air, or on the sea, including firing missiles, the president shall, from that point-in-time, have ninety-days to request authorization from Congress to continue the use of military force. The Congress shall then have ninety-days to authorize the president to continue to use military force. The Congress must vote yes or no within this period. If the president does not make the request in a timely fashion or Congress does not approve the use of military force, the military must be withdrawn as quickly as the safety of the troops allows. If Congress fails to vote on the action, this shall be considered an act of treason and all members of Congress who decline to vote shall be arrested and tried for same. Those willing to vote shall do so.

4.2 The President of the United States as the Chief Executive of the United States shall have the authority to issue Executive Orders to implement the laws of our nation and to safeguard the freedoms of our people. Congress may halt the execution of any Executive Order with a successful majority vote in both Houses under regular order.

4.3 The President may be impeached for treason, bribery, high crimes, and misdemeanors, and significant violations of the Emoluments Clause, including enriching himself or his family through his actions as president. Twenty-five percent of the Senate or of the House of Representatives may request an investigation of the president by the investigating authority. Upon receiving a report from the investigating authority that grounds for impeachment exist, the Senate will conduct hearings and proceed to a vote on the impeachment issue. A majority vote shall result in impeachment and removal of the president from office.

4.4 The President's power of pardon may not be utilized to pardon himself, the vice president, the director of any federal agency, or any individual being investigated or found guilty of any crimes connected to the executive branch.

The Supreme Court

Section 5: Proposals to achieve intended outcomes

Section 5.1 sets forth standards for removing a justice from the Supreme Court.

5.1 The Supreme Court of the United States may have a justice removed from the Court for treason, bribery, high crimes, and misdemeanors, including a finding of misappropriation of office through unfair process in appointment. Review of any justice may be requested by a majority vote of Congress, by the president, or may be taken on by the investigating authority without any outstanding request, but by an initial review of the justice that indicates a valid reason for removal may exist.

Although I am not suggesting it at this time, setting a term of appointment of less than lifetime should well be considered in the future.

Office of Ombudsman

Section 6: Proposals to achieve intended outcomes

Sections 6.1 through 6.8 establish the Office of Ombudsman to ensure that necessary legal review of possible crimes by elected officials can be properly conducted with a minimum of political influence and interference. Refusing to testify or defying a subpoena will not be allowed. Claims of executive privilege or protecting other investigations from exposure need be of no concern when the investigating authority is not political and may hear evidence in private and maintain it in private if appropriate.

6.1 The Office of Ombudsman shall be created as the investigating authority of the United States. It shall be the responsibility of this office to ensure good and faithful service to the United States by all members and staff of the executive, judiciary, and legislative branches of the government.

6.2 The Supreme Court shall appoint a nine-member Ombudsman Commission to oversee the Office of Ombudsman. The appointment shall be as follows: for the initial appointment, the Chief Justice shall appoint one individual to a five-year term, the next four ranking judges in terms of their date of appointment to the Court shall each appoint one individual to a four-year term, the remaining four judges shall each appoint one individual to a three-year term. Thereafter, all appointments shall be to a five-year term. As judges retire from the Supreme Court, their replacements shall inherit the slot on the Commission held by their predecessors in terms of appointment to the Commission and shall continue with the responsibility for that appointment.

6.3 The Ombudsman Commission shall oversee but not direct the Office of Ombudsman. They shall select and appoint an Ombudsman who shall be the Executive Director of the office. His term shall be of an indeterminate tenure. He may be dismissed by a vote of five of the Ombudsman Commissioners. The Ombudsman shall direct the overall operation of the office.

6.4 The Ombudsman shall appoint, with the approval of the Ombudsman Commission, three Deputy Ombudsmen. One each, for each branch of the government—executive, judicial, and legislative. Review of concerns and investigation of possible issues in each branch shall be under their direction. They will also assist the Ombudsman in directing the overall operation of the Office of Ombudsman.

6.5 The Ombudsman shall have full powers of subpoena without the approval of any court being required. The power of subpoena will not be restricted by any claims of executive privilege or secrecy in the name of national security. The Ombudsman shall have the power to compel testimony by witnesses. They will not lose the right to claim protection from providing information for fear of self-recrimination. However, any such claim will require negotiation of providing information with immunity, limited or total. That decision will remain with the Ombudsman as to the necessity of obtaining the information versus the value of lessening appropriate accountability. The Ombudsman shall have the power to compel the Attorney General, the F.B.I., and the C.I.A. to assist in any investigation.

6.6 All investigations by the Ombudsman shall remain secret during the conduct of said investigation. Upon completion of a given investigation, a report will be made to the Ombudsman Commission, including the prosecutorial direction intended and the information that may be made public without endangering national security or public safety or the conduct of an intended prosecution. Such report shall be reviewed by the Ombudsman Commission, and it shall determine what shall be released to the public at that time. Any leaks that occur and any attempts to access the content of the investigation while it is on-going may be prosecuted as felonies.

6.7 Any member of the executive, judicial, or legislative branches of government may request an investigation by the Ombudsman. It shall be strictly up to the discretion of the Ombudsman as to whether an investigation should be conducted. The Ombudsman may also determine to initiate an investigation at his/her own discretion.

6.8 The Ombudsman may be impeached for treason, bribery, high crimes, or misdemeanors if a combined vote of the Chief Justice, the president, and the majority and minority leaders of the Senate and the House of Representatives acting as a convening authority vote to do so. They shall appoint a Special Prosecutor to conduct an investigation. Said Special Prosecutor shall have the same powers of investigation as the Ombudsman for the purposes of the investigation. The completed investigation will be reviewed by the Convening Authority and they will decide whether or not to impeach the Ombudsman. This amendment will have a significant impact on moving the United States back to the pursuit of an honest path towards reestablishing a country where the right to "Life, Liberty, and the pursuit of Happiness" belongs to every individual, and is cherished and protected as a right that belongs to every human from the moment he or she is born. It accomplishes this by removing or altering many of the structural aspects of our government's organization, which have been built up over two-hundred-and-thirty-years to allow the attainment and retaining of power to be the actual function of government, rather than serving the people of the country.

This, however, is an effective vaccination to help reduce the current abuses of power.

It is not a cure.

PART 4

IMMEDIATE SOLUTIONS TO IMMEDIATE PROBLEMS

UNIVERSAL HEALTH CARE

"Disease, sickness, and old age touch every family. Tragedy doesn't ask who you voted for. Health care is a basic human right."

— Elizabeth Warren, Massachusetts Senator

There are several issues that cannot wait for the process. They must be dealt with now, through separate amendments to The Constitution. What I propose are potential workable solutions to address our most pressing issues.

The first and most important of these issues is Universal Health Care. Without provision of Universal Health Care, we are in effect a caste system society. And if we do not provide basic health care for all existing human beings in our country, then none of the claims we make about American freedom and our commitment to "Life, Liberty and the pursuit of Happiness" are sustainable. Our founding fathers understood this, even if they did not immediately implement all aspects of it when they wrote the following words and established them as integral to our constitution.

"We the people of the United States, in Order to form a more perfect Union, establish Justice, insure domestic Tranquility, provide for the common defence, promote the general Welfare, and secure the Blessings of Liberty to ourselves and our Posterity, do ordain and establish this Constitution for the United States of America."

If we truly intend to "promote the general Welfare," then maintaining Universal Health Care as a way to provide a specified package of benefits to all members of society with the end goal of providing financial risk protection, improved access to health services, and improved health outcomes is the logical next step to take.

The arguments against adapting Universal Health Care include:

It is too expensive.

FACT: Per data from the Office of Management and Budget, the cost of health care for the next ten years will be forty-nine trillion dollars with twenty-nine million uninsured. The cost of Medicare for the next ten years would be thirty-two trillion dollars with zero uninsured. Universal Health Care will be less expensive, which is why so many countries decide to keep it.

You will die waiting for care.

FACT: You will certainly die waiting for care if you are uninsured. If you have the same health care as everyone else however you have at least the same chance to receive the proper treatment to remain alive.

The real problem is that patient numbers are rapidly increasing as the population increases. Meanwhile the cost of a medical education has reduced the number of trained physicians who are natural born citizens. Visit any hospital and you will find a great number of the medical staff are of foreign descent. This is not a criticism of these professionals, only of our government's support in regard to the health needs of our country.

The quality of care is worse

FACT: The quality of not getting any care is certainly worse. Not only is there no evidence that Universal Health Care reduces the quality of care, there are numerous studies that indicate a significant satisfaction with the level of health care available in countries that provide universal health care.

Countries with Universal Health Care and year of implementation

COUNTRY	YEAR OF IMPLEMENTATION
Australia	1975
Austria	1967
Bahrain	1957
Belgium	1945
Brunei	1958
Canada	1966
Cyprus	1980
Denmark	1973
Finland	1972
France	1974
Germany	1941
Greece	1983
Hong Kong	1993
Iceland	1990
Ireland	1977
Isreal	1955
Italy	1978
Japan	1938
Kuwait	1950
Luxembourg	1973
Netherlands	1966
New Zealand	1938
Norway	1912
Portugal	1979
Singapore	1993
Slovenia	1972
South Korea	1988
Spain	1986
Sweden	1955
Switzerland	1994
United Arab Emirates	1971
United Kingdom	1948

Every industrialized nation in the world has had Universal Health Care for at least twenty-two years to one-hundred-and-five years. Not a single one has found a reason to abandon it. For the record, recent protests in the United Kingdom regarding Universal Health Care were focused on what the government was attempting to change, not on whether or not it should be abandoned. Other beliefs about Universal Health Care that are simply not true include:

Universal Health Care is less efficient.

FALSE, refer to the points noted above.

The quality of care is worse.

FALSE, according to Forbes magazine,

"It's fairly well accepted that the U.S. has the most expensive healthcare system in the world, but many continue to falsely assume that we pay more for healthcare because we get better healthcare, or better health outcomes. The evidence, however, clearly does not support that view.

The World Health Organization recently classified the United States as 37th out of 190 countries in the world."

Universal Health Care will make it nearly impossible for Wall Street, Big Pharma, major medical corporations, and the insurance industry to make huge financial killings from sick people.

ABSOLUTELY TRUE! This is an on-going problem. Don't think so? Consider the following:

The Fall of Prozac and the Rise of Xigris

Let's look at how costs for medication was determined by one company, Eli Lilly. In 2000, when Lilly was waging a court battle aimed at protecting their antidepressant medicine Prozac from generic competition, it lost the case and its stock price dropped by more than 30% in anticipation of Prozac's patent expiring in August of 2001. This was a huge blow to Lilly considering Prozac sales earned as much as $2.6 billion a year and that equaled only a quarter of its revenue.

The impact was immediate, Frances Leath, a former executive involved in the pricing strategy recalls, "There was a huge amount of external pressure to get earnings back up and the stock price along with them." "Inside the company you had staff saying, 'We just lost $2 billion a year. Am I going to get laid off?"

Then, just two months after Prozac lost its U.S. patent, the company had a big win. The Food and Drug Administration green-lighted Xigris, a drug that in clinical trials was proving to be effective at treating severe sepsis. Each year 225,000 people were being killed by sepsis and they had no approved drug to fight it. By then, Lilly's leadership had spent several months discussing a potential price for Xigris.

Leath recalls a preliminary consensus forming around a price of about $500 per dose. That was no bargain, that price tag was one hundred times more than the company's manufacturing cost and at the higher range of the medicine's class. But with Prozac's sales plummeting and the medical community's excitement about Xigris, that price began to seem inadequate. "All of a sudden, the price everyone talked about was $10,000 per dose." "Someone just pulled that figure out of their derriere, and then it became the number." (Facebook post by Frances Leath)

Turing Pharmaceuticals *(Sourced from Martin Shrkeli Wikipedia)*

Turing Pharmaceuticals was founded in February 2015 by Martin Shkreli and launched with three drugs.

- An intranasal version of Oxytocin
- An intranasal version of Ketamine to treat depression
- Vecamyl to treat hypertension

The business strategy Shkreli implemented involved obtaining out-of-patent medications, in lieu of developing new medicines to introduce into the marketplace. Each new drug acquired by Turing would undergo pricing evaluations to maximize profits for the new venture. This strategy worked well given it was operating in a niche market with limited competition. This meant that instead of investing in the expensive regulatory process for the development of a new generic drug, the company could acquire an out-of-patent drug at a fairly non-competitive price. The inevitable result was a higher price for the drugs Turig sold.

In June 2015, just months preceding Turing's acquisition of Impax Laboratories' drug, Daraprim (pyrimethamine) a medication used primarily as an anti-malarial and anti-parasitic but also in conjunction with Leucovorin and Sulfadiazine to treat the symptoms suffered by AIDs patients, there was a change in the drug's distribution model. When Daraprim expired there was no generic version of it available and Turing required that Daraprim be removed from distribution to both wholesalers and pharmacies. As a result, Impax made a move toward tightly controlled distribution and Turing opted for closed distribution which would ensure the high pricing strategy Turing was after. The New York Times noted that the deal "made send only if Turing planned to raise the price of the drug substantially."

On September 17, 2015, a little over a month after the deal closed, Dave Muoio of Healio, an in-depth clinical information website for health care professionals reported on a letter from the Infectious Diseases Society of America and the HIV Medicine Association to executives at Turing, and questioned the new pricing for Daraprim. By this time, the price for one dose of the drug on the U.S. market had increased from $13.50 to $750, in other words a factor of 56. However, despite intense pressure, Turing declined to reduce the price of the drug.

On October 22, 2015, Mark L. Baum, CEO of Imprimis Pharmaceuticals, announced that his company would bring to market a cheaper and more efficient alternative to Daraprim. Baum noted, "This is not the first time a sole supply generic drug—especially one that has been approved for use as long as Daraprim — has had its price increased suddenly and to a level that may make it unaffordable." Baum announced the availability of Daraprim's $1 per dose alternative as part of a larger corporate program "Imprimus Cares" to make "novel and customizable medicines available to physicians and patients at accessible prices." Today, the cost for the Daraprim alternative, oral formulations of pyrimethamine and leucovorin, start at $99 for a 100 count bottle, essentially, one dollar per dose.

The response by Turing on November 23, 2015, was not to reduce the list price of Daraprim but to offer hospitals volume discounts of 50%. Turing issued a statement that it was not as important to cut the list price as it was to reduce the cost to hospitals where most patients would receive their initial treatments. The company pledged that no patient needing Daraprim would ever be denied access to it. Infectious disease specialists and patient advocates, including Tim Horn of the Treatment Action Group and Carlos del Rio of the HIV Medicine Association, didn't think this was enough, given most patients require continued treatment weeks and months after being discharged from the hospital.

The Current Administration's Role

Erin Meershon in his articles wrote,

"He rails against the drug industry. But Trump is turning to his ranks to fill the administration."

"His Food and Drug Administration Chief, Scott Gottlieb, was a longtime industry investor and adviser to major players like GlaxoSmithKline and Bristol-Myers Squibb. A senior adviser at the Health and Human Services Department, Keagan Lenihan, joined the administration after running the lobby shop for the drug and distribution giant McKesson. And Trump has a former Gilead lobbyist, Joe Grogan, reviewing health care regulations at the Office of Management and Budget. The chief of staff at HHS, Lance Leggitt, lobbied for a whole host of drug clients, even last year."

"This week the president named Alex Azar, who spent more than a decade at the pharmaceutical giant Eli Lilly, as his health secretary nominee."

The latter development puts the pharmaceutical industry in charge of regulating its own exorbitant pricing. Although, Azar's career history would make him seem relatively innocuous. He's a Yale educated lawyer who clerked for Antonin Scalia on the Supreme Court. He was also general counsel and deputy assistant secretary of the Department of Health and Human Services under President George W. Bush. He then moved on to serve as vice president and president of Lilly USA, LLC, one of the biggest pharmaceutical corporations in the country–one that is notorious for raising the price of its insulin products by more than 1,000 percent since 1994. During his tenure at Eli Lilly, the list price of Humalog insulin increased by 345 percent from just over $2,600 to more than $9,000. While price gouging consumers, the company spent millions to lobby Congress, the Department of Health and Human Services, and other administrative agencies. In 2016 alone they spent $5.7 million.

Azar has been quoted saying that patients pay too much for prescription drugs, then on the flip side, he's talked about the role of insurers and prescription benefit managers in ensuring the high cost of drugs. His decision to join Eli Lilly's staff was questionable at the time, especially given he had previously been an administrator overseeing investigations into the corporation's creation of marketing materials for the unapproved use of one of their products.

Eli Lilly is also named in a class-action lawsuit, which alleges that the corporation colluded with Novo Nordisk and Sanofi in order to keep the U.S. insulin market prices increasing over time. Much of the activity in the case occurred during Azar's time as President of Eli Lilly, USA.

Azar's statements on drug pricing reveal a bias towards Big Pharma. When asked about drug prices at the Versa Summit on May 8, 2017, he avoided addressing price controls and limitations on high drug prices, or even admitting the prescription drug industry's role in setting high drug prices. He pointed to the insurance industry as a culprit.

He has also called for lower barriers of regulation and safety for prescription drugs in multiple remarks, saying that regulators have set an "unrealistically high bar for new innovations to clear." Public support for lowering drug prices is at an all-time high, with Americans from both major parties backing the idea to lower drug prices. Even Donald Trump has repeatedly called for reform, calling out prescription drug corporations for "getting away with murder."

Azar's resume lists his experiences in both the private and public sectors of healthcare, and to some that resume may make him a more competent choice for HHS Secretary than his predecessor. His major conflict of interest and previous statements suggest he is not prepared to run the agency that could work towards lowering drug prices, a top issue for many Americans. His nomination to Health and Human Services undercuts the administration's message on lowering drug prices, and the Senate should not confirm Azar to that role. (Justin Mendoza, organizer for Public Citizen's Access to Medicines program article)

How bad is U.S. Healthcare?

Newsweek published an article on July 7, 2017 titled, "How Bad Is U.S. Healthcare? Among high-income nations it's the worst, study says.

Among the 11 developed nations, the U.S. healthcare system received the worst rating by the Commonwealth Fund, an organization who conducts an evaluation every three years. The countries included in the evaluation include: Australia, Canada, France, Germany, the Netherlands, New Zealand, Norway, Sweden, Switzerland, the United Kingdom and the United States.

Countries were ranked by:
- healthcare process
- access to healthcare
- administrative efficiency
- equity
- healthcare outcomes

In addition to ranking last or close to last in access, administrative efficiency, equity and healthcare outcomes, the U.S. was found to spend the most money on healthcare. One of the poorest ratings received was for equality of coverage. The report found that 44% of low-income Americans have trouble gaining access to coverage compared with 26% of high-income Americans. The numbers for the U.K.

were 7% and 4%, respectively. In addition, the U.K.'s National Health Service was deemed the best healthcare system, just as it was in 2014.

The report reads, "In contrast to the U.S., over the last decade the U.K. saw a larger decline in mortality amenable to health care than the other countries studied." Though the U.S. ranked fifth in care process, which includes, prevention, safe care, coordination, and patient engagement, its overall score was easily the worst of the 11 nations.

The report also states that the U.S. is the only high-income nation to lack Universal Health Care and that the effects of this go beyond just access issues. Administrative efficiency, for example, lags because of time wasted sorting out billing and insurance claims. The Commonwealth Fund concludes that for the country's healthcare system to compete with those of other high-income nations, a drastic change in course is necessary.

Some actions may include:

- improving primary care offerings
- moving away from fee-for-service payments
- introducing incentives that can lead to the better coordination of care
- supporting and perhaps modeling organizations who excel at the coordination of healthcare

For the record, in 2014, the Think Tank also rated the U.S. healthcare system as the worst-performing of the nations analyzed.

Justifications for Universal Health Care

Provide for the common defense

An unhealthy nation is obviously less able to defend itself. Poor health may severely impact a nation's ability to establish and maintain adequate productivity during the need for being on a "war-time footing."

Provide for general welfare

We need to promote the general welfare of the country. Even if you are healthy, you are impacted by those who are sick. When you consider how the plague wiped out more than twenty-two million, almost one third of a continent's population, it becomes increasingly important to rely on immunization as a way to reduce the spread of infection to those who are unprotected, to those who have been properly protected and to those who are unable to be protected. Only recently we experienced a measles epidemic and every year we are encouraged to protect ourselves against the flu.

Secure the blessings of liberty to ourselves and to our posterity

Let's face it—the real concern for Universal Health Care is what its cost will be to the individual. There are ways to make the cost acceptable and even a bargain.

1. Ensure everyone, including wealthy individuals and corporations, pay a fair share. This means if you make more money than others, you pay a bigger share of the cost than others.

2. You control the cost of everybody's share by controlling the cost of healthcare. Hospitals routinely charge hundreds of times the actual cost of supplies in part because they are, for the most part, run to earn a profit. If you do not believe this can work, have a look at Medicare. There is a significant difference between the amount hospitals want to charge, and what they have to accept under the law.

Human Decency

We simply ought to care enough for each other not to allow unnecessary suffering and death. If you think you should not have to pay your fair share for this, then explain why you should be allowed to drive on the roads others have built? attend schools you did not create? travel on buses, trains, and planes you did not construct? and live in peace you have not paid for with service in the military?

Arguments in favor of adopting Universal Health Care include:

Everyone is included
No one needs to suffer or die due to a lack of access to healthcare

An economic boon
We all benefit by eliminating insurance costs and making coverage portable for employees. In this way, we can level out the cost of healthcare, place large and small business on equal footing. Healthier employees leads to less time off for sick leave and increased productivity.

Uniform benefits
You should receive the same treatment as your senator or congressman. Across the board healthcare with a focus on health and not profit would enhance the focus on prevention and/or early detection and treatment. A healthier nation will be stronger and less susceptible to natural epidemics or biological attacks.

Effective Models in Operations
The thirty-six industrialized nations currently using Universal Health Care can serve as ideal models for best to implement our own system and not needing to re-invent the wheel.

Financial Risk Protection
One huge positive outcome is an economic one. Number of people who go bankrupt every year because of medical bills:

Britain	0
Canada	0
France	0
Japan	0
Germany	0
Netherlands	0
Switzerland	0
United States	$643,300

AMENDMENT TO THE CONSTITUTION TO IMPLEMENT UNIVERSAL HEALTHCARE

If we do not provide Universal Health Care, we cannot claim any real commitment to the right to life for the wealthy or the poor. The poor will die from lack of healthcare. The rich will die because they do not exist in isolation, and money will protect them only for so long. Further, if we do not protect the right to life, which is the basic right on which all other rights rely, then nothing of what we claim about our country carries any legitimate meaning. I do not claim to have all of the answers, but I have the basic one. We live, or we perish together. If we do not protect life, our country will end.

1.1 The United States government shall be required to provide access to health care with a specified package of benefits to all human beings within the United States and its territories.

1.2 The package of benefits for all existing human beings shall include, but not necessarily be limited to, all medical services: necessary to save life; necessary to prevent deterioration of health; necessary to cure and prevent the spread of disease; necessary to allow a healthy condition of living (including dental, optical, and hearing); necessary to enable handicapped individuals to maximize their opportunities to participate fully in life; and necessary to care properly for those who are disabled and unable to care for themselves. This shall include: Allopathic, Naturopathic, Homeopathic, Chiropractic, Acupuncture, Traditional Chinese Medicine, Ayurvedic Medicine, and Clinical Nutrition.

1.3 Medical decisions shall be left to the purview of individuals and their doctors. Voluntary medical operations not essential to the elements listed in 1.2 such as cosmetic surgery purely for the sake of appearance and not related to restoring health shall not fall under Universal Health Care.

1.4 The term "existing human beings" shall not apply to a human fetus unless the medical procedure in question can be conducted within the womb or unless the fetus can survive outside the womb, which would make a procedure within the womb prohibitive.

NOTE: Abortion will be an acceptable and covered procedure and will not be subject to arbitrary restrictions such as fetal heartbeat being evidence that the fetus should be recognized as a human being. The basis of this position is the founding fathers' stated belief that the government will recognize everyone has the right to "Life, Liberty, and the pursuit of Happiness." If a human being has the right to life, he/she has the right to choose to end his/her life. If not, the phrase "right to life" is not truthful. Rather, it means you have a limited right, and someone else will determine that; therefore, someone else owns that right. However, if he/she may choose to end his/her life, then he/she obviously has the right to choose to do whatever else with his/her body that does not injure another existing human being. Bodily autonomy places the right of an existing human being over that of a fetus.

1.5 Procedures or medicine involving birth prevention are covered under this amendment.

1.6 A portion of the funds raised for the Universal Health Care system shall be dedicated to health education, including sexual education in our schools. All such education will be on a strictly scientific basis.

1.7 A portion of the funds raised for the Universal Health Care system shall be used to educate individuals qualified by intelligence and skill for the medical profession at no financial cost to them to cover tuition and instruction materials. The cost for such training shall be reimbursed by the individual through service in the Universal Health Care system wherever assigned for an appropriate number of years determined by the level of education, with a minimum of two years for the lowest level of education, progressing upward for higher levels of education.

1.8 A portion of the funds raised for the Universal Health Care system shall be used for the construction and staffing of medical facilities including but not limited to: hospitals, clinics, and emergency response. Veterans Administration Medical Centers shall remain under the direction of the Veterans Administration who is equipped to focus on both the general medical needs of veterans and the specific areas of debilitating physical and mental injuries common to veterans.

1.9 All prescribed medicines shall be covered under the Universal Health Care plan. The United States government shall negotiate reasonable prices with pharmaceutical companies, under which a reasonable return on their investment will not impinge on the ability of individuals to receive medications or cause a cessation in developing new drugs and new treatments. If necessary, the United States government may take control of facilities and draft personnel to ensure the continued growth of needed medical solutions.

1.10 The Universal Health Care system shall be paid for by everyone as follows:

Earned Income	Percentage Assessment	Amount paid on maximum earned level	Accumulated maximum paid at maximum earned level
0 — 20,000	0.5%	$100	$100
20,001 — 50,000	2%	$400	$500
50,001 — 100,000	2.3%	$1,150	$1,650
100,001 — 150,000	2.5%	$1,250	$2,900
150,001 — 200,000	3%	$1,500	$4,400
200,001 — 250,000	4%	$2,000	$6,400
250,001 — 450,000	5%	$10,000	$16,400
450,001 — 750,000	7.5%	$150,000	$38,900
750,001 — 1,000,000	9%	$100,000	$138,900
1,000,001 — 2,000,000	10%	$150,000	$188,900
2,000,001 — 3,000,000	15%	$200,000	$388,900
3,000,001 — 4,000,000	20%	$400,000	$788,900
4,000,001 — 5,000,000	20%	$400,000	$1,388,900

Add 20% ($400,000) to the Accumulated Maximum per each additional $1,000,000

- Exempted from taxation on earned income: Social Security disbursements, disability disbursements, Veterans Administrations disbursements, and child support payments, whether from government or private sources.

- 90% tax on all money housed outside of the United States, unless within a year of the passage of this amendment the money is accurately reported to the IRS, and all other taxes that would be paid on earned income plus the required amount for the Universal Health Care system is paid per the schedule of payments.

- All corporations shall pay 10% on gross earnings, including earnings credited outside of the United States. All employers shall pay 5% of their total payroll for the year, including bonuses or any other cash disbursements.

NOTE: It should not be included in a constitutional amendment, however, all tax breaks afforded to individuals who generally earn an income above $500,000 should be eliminated from the Tax Code, along with all tax breaks to corporations who pay virtually zero taxes.

Finally, the government shall control the costs for all medical processes and procedures to prevent overcharging and ensure appropriate funding for the Health Care system.

EQUAL RIGHTS

"We are confronted with a moral issue...
whether all Americans are to be afforded equal rights
and equal opportunities, whether we are going to
treat our fellow Americans as we want to be treated."

— John F. Kennedy

The second issue we must address is equal rights. It is simply insufficient to support the right to "Life, Liberty, and the pursuit of Happiness" if we do not ensure those rights are required to apply equally to all.

We live in a time where women struggle for equal pay and equal opportunity for advancement. We are witnessing extensive revelations of sexual abuse at the highest government and corporate levels.

Richard Pryor, the comedian spoke of visiting a prison and speaking with the "brothers." He asked one man who had murdered four innocent people in their home, "Why did you do it?" The response, "They was there" is both hilarious and tragic.

Much the same response is used against the women who are victims:

"It was their fault."

"It was caused by the way she dressed."

"It was because of the way she behaved."

A partial listing of the public figures accused of sexual misconduct from Time magazine, updated online January 26, 2018

Ray Moore, former Chief Justice of the Alabama Supreme Court–twice; a defeated conservative candidate for senator in one of the deepest red states

Harvey Weinstein, a powerful film mogul with his own successful company

Steve Wynn, Chairman and CEO of Wynn Resorts; RNC Finance Chair

Ross Levinsohn, CEO and Publisher of *The Los Angeles Times*

Corey Lewandoski, Campaign Manager for presidential candidate Donald Trump

Andrea Ramsey, a Democratic congressional candidate in Kansas

Jack Latvala, a Republican state senator in Florida

Jerry Richardson, owner, NFL Carolina Panthers

Tavis Smiley, host of the Tavis Smiley Show

Dan Johnson, Kentucky state representative

Ron Lizza, Washington correspondent for *The New Yorker*

Mario Batali, celebrity chef

Jon Heely, Director of Music Publishing, Disney

Alex Kozinski, U.S. Appeals Court judge

Trent Franks, Republican representative, U. S. House of Representatives, Arizona

Harold Ford, Jr., Morgan Stanley, former Democratic representative, U.S. House of Representatives, Tennessee

Dylan Howard, Chief Content officer, America Media, Inc., which includes *The National Enquirer*

James Levine, Metropolitan Opera Conductor

Ruben Kihuen, Democratic representative, U.S. House of Representatives, Nevada

Blake Farenthold, Republican representative, U.S. House of Representatives, Texas

Ben Affleck, actor, Oscar-winning director

Geraldo Rivera, political commentator

Israel Horowitz, playwright and director

Matt Lauer, host, *Today Show*

John Conyers, Democratic representative, U.S. House of Representatives, Michigan

Charlie Rose, host, *Charlie Rose Show*

Glenn Thrush, *N.Y. Times*, White House correspondent

Jameis Winston, quarterback, FL Tampa Bay Buccaneers

Al Franken, Democratic senator, Minnesota

Eddie Berganza, editor, DC Comics

Louis C.K., comedian, actor

Dan Schoen, Democratic state representative, Minnesota

Steven Seagal, actor

Kevin Spacey, actor

Hamilton Fish, president and publisher, *The New Republic*

Mark Halperin, journalist

George H.W. Bush, president

Roman Polanski, director.

R. Kelly, rapper

Chris Savino, Nickelodeon

David Blaine, magician

Roy Price, head, Amazon Studios

Oliver Stone, director

Others facing similar accusations but not included in the *Time Magazine* list include:

Rob Porter, White House Staff Secretary

Bill Clinton, president

Stephen Bittel, former Democratic Party Chairman for Florida

Tony Cornish, Republican state representative, Minnesota

Jeff Hoover, Republican, Kentucky House Speaker

Tim Nolan, Trump Campaign Chair, Campbell County, Kentucky

A more recent addition to this list would include the following Trump appointment:

Brett Kavanugh, Associate Justice of the United States Supreme Court

Jeffrey Epstein, wealthy financier and friend of Trump

Corruption & The Pursuit of Power

It is evident that all human organizations evolve into something other than intended due to the pursuit of power and often the result is corruption. Sexual abuse should be added as a form of such corruption. The list above may contain some people who are innocent, but all of them are people of power and influence. The unequal treatment of women has resulted in the false beliefs that they are there for the taking and that it is acceptable to pay them less than their male counterparts for the same work. The inequality of women must cease, or there can be no such thing as "Life, Liberty and the pursuit of Happiness" for all.

However, women are not the only ones who suffer from inequality. The issue of race is a constant one when we consider the challenges we face in regard to inequality. And while blacks suffer from this form of discrimination more than other minorities, racism inevitably affects all races.

Racism

Blacks have gone through slavery, Jim Crow, and they have struggled for the right to defend their country in combat, and to fight for civil rights. The current racial tensions resulting from police killing unarmed, non-threatening blacks and walking away without any sense of responsibility are quickly mounting as evidenced by the president's response to a recent non-violent protest during a public event. Taking a knee at a public event, has been turned a protest against our flag and an action of disrespect to our military, and at the direction of our president.

Other minorities such as Hispanics are denigrated by this president as "Mexican rapists" and frequently accorded second-class citizenship in our society. Asians too, though perceived as more polite and in many cases fairly intelligent, still suffer from inequality in treatment.

Perhaps no one has suffered more from racial inequality than Native Americans. For all of the white history on this continent, their story has been one of being eliminated.

Even the holocaust does not approach the massive genocide inflicted on Native Americans by the white European invasion. Millions were killed, land was stolen, and cultures were destroyed. Even today, land that has been preserved as sacred is being sold off for development and private profit. Inequality based on race must cease, or there can be no such thing as "Life, Liberty and the pursuit of Happiness" for all.

Gender & Sexuality

Another area where people suffer inequality is gender and sexuality. If you are a heterosexual male or female, it is difficult to absorb the idea that another person who is physically identical to you may wish to live as a different gender or pursue a different path of sexuality. Your lack of understanding does not mean you may treat someone as unequal.

Equality lies in how we treat people, not in whether we can perform in a superior manner for a given action such as throwing a javelin. That may have been important in providing food on the African Savannah hundreds of thousands of years ago. It does not make the better thrower superior in how they deserve to be treated.

In terms of gender, science has begun to make it very clear that gender preference is not simply a choice. The human body is an engine with multiple components of which we do not possess a full understanding, both in how they work and how they interact with our mind and our experiences in living. In this circumstance it is a facetious act to treat someone who is not the same as oneself as being unequal.

Where does this idea come from, that you must be the same as me, or I as you to be treated equally? Inequality based on gender preference or sexual choice must also cease.

To clarify, no sexual act should occur between one or more people unless it is a consensual act acceptable to all involved. "Consensual" meaning all who are involved are in agreement and are capable of such consent; "capable" means they are of an adult age, they are not mentally incapacitated by physical limitations or by induced chemicals such as drugs or alcohol; "involved" includes any witnesses who did not choose to be a witness such as might occur by having sex in public or public "flashing" of genitals; all involved have the right to withdraw their consent and, in such a case, the activity involving them must cease as promptly as possible; and finally, consent of all involved in the act does not alleviate a commitment to another not present in the form of marital bonds or similar agreement.

The Role of Religion

At this point, we need to discuss a major tool used to justify inflicting inequality. That tool is often described as inner conscience, or more commonly religious belief. Covered extensively in recent news is the case of a bakery that refused to make a wedding cake for a gay couple. They based their refusal on the argument that to bake the cake would be a violation of their personal religious beliefs.

If that argument is allowed under law, what would have prevented, for example, a diner in a southern state to refuse service to Martin Luther King, Jr. because it would have violated their religious belief in a god who would also classify black humans as less than white ones? The Bible was often used in defense of slavery during the Civil War to assert the inferiority of the black race and frequently since. Martin Luther King, Jr. was arrested for attempting to attend a sit-in at a diner. The religious defense was not used because Jim Crow laws, based in part on religious beliefs already covered the situation.

There is also the well-known case of Kimberly Jean Davis, the county clerk for Rowan County, Kentucky who refused to issue a marriage license to a gay couple. She defied a US federal court order and was embroiled in a lawsuit over the issue until Kentucky made a change in the law, and the lawsuit was dismissed. Subsequently, a federal judge ordered Kentucky to pay $224,000 in legal fees.

Think about that. A clerk refuses to do her job, discriminates on the basis of sexual preference, causes a minor change in the law to avoid a similar situation in the future, and not only costs the citizens of Kentucky the legal costs of defending her, but also the legal fees for the defendants.

Bay View, Michigan is a seasonal resort community. Its community association's by-laws prohibit ownership unless you are a Christian. This must be certified by a letter from a Christian minister testifying to your active participation in a church. A lawsuit claims the community is in clear violation of constitutional, civil, and religious rights, not to mention federal housing rights.

The policy has prevented homeowners from passing the property down to children who are not practicing Christians and prevents purchase of a property by non-Christians. Religious beliefs substituting for the law have long been a problem in the United States, where we proclaim religious freedom and condemn other nations whose government operates under religious authority.

On February 6, 2018, the Attorney General made changes to the policy manuals for U.S. Attorneys' Offices and Department of Justice (DOJ) litigation offices, without any substantive policy announcement. These offices are now required to assign a staff member to monitor all litigation and immediately inform high-ranking political appointees at DOJ whenever the offices are subject to a lawsuit involving religious liberty, when religious liberty is used as a defense in litigation, or when the offices file a suit involving religious liberty.

This took place two weeks after the Trump administration created the Conscience and Religious Freedom Division within the Office for Civil Rights at the Department of Health and Human Services. This new division is charged with shielding medical professionals who, because of their own religious objections, refuse to treat patients.

Hillsdale, Utah shares a staff with Colorado City, Arizona. While the area has a population that is largely populated by those who participate in the Fundamentalist Church of Jesus Christ of Latter Day Saints, particularly in Utah, a recent election resulted in four commissioners being elected who were not FDLS, including a woman. This was the first time non-FDLS individuals were ever elected. Eleven staff members resigned. This included one staff member who said his religious belief did not allow him to follow a woman and forbade him from serving on a board with apostates.

This was the appropriate thing for them to do. If their religious beliefs forbade them from doing the job, resigning from the job seemed the logical next step. The inappropriate thing to do is to stay in the position and refuse to do the job.

Inner conscience or religious belief as an excuse for treating others unequally must cease, or there can be no such thing as "Life, Liberty and the pursuit of Happiness" for all.

AMENDMENT TO THE CONSTITUTION TO IMPLEMENT EQUAL RIGHTS

1. Equality of rights under the law shall not be abridged by the United States or by any state on account of sex, race, gender identification, sexual orientation, or religious belief or non-belief.

2. Inner conscience or religious belief shall not be a defense for refusal to provide a service for which payment is given.

3. The Congress shall have the duty and power to enforce, by appropriate legislation, the provisions of this article.

4. This amendment shall take effect with the first opening or resumption of any congressional session after the date of ratification.

SOCIAL SECURITY

"We will keep the promise of Social Security by taking the responsible steps to strengthen it — not by turning it over to Wall Street."

— Barack Obama

The third issue we must deal with is the "bankrupt" Social Security system. Social Security is entirely self-financed. It has no connection to the national debt. According to the Social Security trustees, it has $2.85 trillion in it. So, the questions are:

How can it be going broke?
What do we need to do to ensure its solvency?
And, what do we need to do to ensure fair and responsible payouts?

In straightforward terms, administration-after-administration has raided the vault. Legally, through what amounts to a pyramid scheme, by disingenuous means, money has been stolen and used for such things as waging wars and making the wealthy more wealthy.

Social Security is the commonly used term for the Federal Old-age, Survivors, and Disability Insurance (OSDI) program. The original Social Security Act was signed into law by President Franklin D. Roosevelt in 1935. The current version of the act, as amended, includes several social welfare and social insurance programs.

A timeline of key developments in the program:

1935 The Social Security Act signed August 14th

1937 The first Social Security Cards issued

1939 Two new categories of beneficiaries added: spouse and minor children of a retired worker

1940 First monthly benefit check issued

1950 Benefits increased / Cost Of Living Adjustments (COLAs) made at irregular intervals (1950 COLA – 77%)

1954 Disability program added to Social Security

1960 *Fleming v Nestor*. Landmark Supreme Court ruling that gave Congress the power to amend and revise the schedule of benefits. The Court also ruled that recipients have no contractual right to receive payments

1961 Early retirement age lowered to 62 with reduced benefits

1965 Medicare health care benefits added to Social Security

1966 Medicare tax of 0.7% added to pay for increased Medicare expenses

1972 Supplementary Security Income (SSI) program federalized and assigned to Social Security Administration

1975 Automatic Cost Of Living Adjustments (COLAs) mandated

1977 COLA adjustments brought back to "sustainable" levels

1983 Taxation of Social Security Benefits introduced; new federal hires required to be under Social Security; retirement age increased for younger workers to 66 and 67 years.

1984 Congress passed the Disabilities Benefits Reform Act, modifying several aspects of the disability programs

1996 Drug addiction or alcoholism disability beneficiaries could no longer be eligible for disability benefits The earnings limit doubled the exemption amount for retired social security beneficiaries. SSI eligibility was terminated for most non-citizens

1997 Temporary Assistance for Needy Families (TANF), replaces Aid to Families With Dependent Children (AFDC) program placed under Social Security Administration

1997 State Children's Health Insurance Program for low income citizens (SCHIP) added to Social Security Administration

2003 Voluntary drug benefits with supplemental Medicare insurance payments from recipients added

2009 No Social Security Benefits for Prisoners Act of 2009 signed

Social Security is funded primarily through payroll taxes called the Federal Insurance Contributions Tax Act (FICA) or Self-Employed Contributions Tax Act (SECA). Tax deposits are collected by the Internal

Revenue Service (IRS) and are formally entrusted to the Federal Old-Age and Survivors insurance Trust Fund and the Federal Disability Insurance Trust Fund, the two Social Security Trust Funds. With a few exceptions, all salaried income, up to an amount specifically determined by law, is subject to the Social Security payroll tax. All income over said amount is not taxed. In 2017, the maximum amount of taxable earnings was $127,200.

Social Security is not going broke, at least technically. Let us review the procedures established by law for handling our money. To do this we can reference the Research Notes & Special Studies by the Historian's Office. However, please note this is an archival or historical document and may not reflect current policies or procedures.

The Financing Procedures — Research Note #20

In the Social Security Act of 1935, the income from the payroll tax was to be credited to a Social Security "account." Benefits were to be paid against this account, but there was no formal trust fund as such. Taxes began to be collected in January 1937, and monthly benefits were to be paid starting in January 1942 (later pushed forward to January 1940). So, the payroll taxes were just credits in the Social Security account on the Treasury's ledger under the initial law.

The investment rules governing payroll tax income were also established in 1935, and are essentially the same ones in use today. Specifically, the 1935 Act stated:

"It shall be the duty of the Secretary of the Treasury to invest such portion of the amounts credited to the Account as is not, in his judgment, required to meet current withdrawals. Such investment may be made only in interest-bearing obligations of the United States or in obligations guaranteed as to both principal and interest by the United States."

In the 1939 Amendments, a formal trust fund was established and a requirement was put in place for annual reports on the actuarial status of the fund. Specifically, the law provided:

"There is hereby created on the books of the Treasury of the United States a trust fund to be known as the 'Federal Old-Age and Survivors Insurance Trust Fund'...the Trust Fund shall consist of the securities held by the Secretary of the Treasury for the Old-Age Reserve Account on the books of the Treasury on January 1, 1940, which securities and amount the Secretary of the Treasury is authorized and directed to transfer to the Trust Fund, and, in addition, such amounts as may be appropriated to the Trust Fund as herein under provided" (Title II, Section 201a)

In other words, a formal trust fund was established for the Social Security program and the credits already on the Treasury's books for the Social Security program were to be transferred to this fund, along with all future revenues raised for the fund.

The investment procedures adopted in 1939 were modified only slightly from those in the original Act of 1935. Basically, changes were made in the interest rate rules governing the investments, and the Managing Trustee was designated as the investing official (who happens to be the Secretary of the Treasury in any case), but in most other respects the language was similar to that in the original law.

Both the 1935 and the 1939 laws specified three types of purchases that might be made:

1) securities on original issue at par;

2) by purchase of outstanding obligations at the market price; and

3) via the issuance of "special obligation bonds" that could be issued only to the Social Security Trust Fund. These special obligation bonds were not to be marketable, although the other two forms of securities could be. The idea of special obligation bonds was not new nor unique to the Social Security program. Similar bonds were used during World War I and World War II, and it was in fact the Second Liberty Bond Act, amended in 1939, that allowed the Social Security program to make use of this type of government

Consequently, over time the Social Security Trust Funds have included a mix of marketable and non-marketable Treasury securities. Over the years, the proportion has shifted heavily in favor of special obligation bonds as the main asset held by the Social Security Trust Funds. Prior to 1960, the Treasury's policy was to invest primarily in marketable securities, although this policy was not always followed. Since 1960, the policy has been to invest principally in special obligation bonds, unless the managing trustee of the funds (i.e., the Secretary of the Treasury) determines that investment in marketable securities would be "in the public interest." In fact, since 1980 no marketable securities have been added to the Trust Funds.

For a more detailed explanation see the Office of the Actuary's Actuarial Note #142

Since the assets in the Social Security Trust Funds consist of Treasury securities, this means that the taxes collected under the Social Security payroll tax are in effect being lent to the federal government to be expended for whatever present purposes the government requires. In this indirect sense, one could say that the Social Security Trust Funds are being spent for non-Social Security purposes. However, all this really means is that the trust funds hold their assets in the form of Treasury securities.

These financing procedures have not changed in any fundamental way since payroll taxes were first collected in 1937. What has changed, however, is the accounting procedures used in federal budgeting when it comes to the Social Security Trust Funds.

As noted above Social Security is not technically broke nor has the government technically stolen our money. As the above report states, "the trust funds hold their assets in the form of Treasury securities." Two of those types of securities are marketable securities, meaning they could be placed on the market and sold for cash.

The other security, which makes up the vast majority of the fund and was the only security used in the last thirty-seven years, is "special obligation bonds." Essentially, they are paper receipts for our money payable only by the federal government. They do require interest payments. Those are also paid in "special obligation bonds."

The latest reports indicate that the Bureau of Public Debt, located in Parkersburg, West Virginia, holds "special obligation bonds" for the Federal Treasury in the amount of 2.85 trillion dollars. The legal and rational conclusion is that Social Security is not broke and no laws have been broken.

The 2016 Annual Report of The Board of Trustees on the system's financial condition states the system is not bankrupt but will face a shortfall in terms of making payments in 2034. They predict the system will be able to fund 79% of disbursements that year. Under current conditions, the projection is they will be able to fund 74% of disbursements through 1990. End Research Note #20

On this basis, a modest increase today could take care of the problem in 2034, when it would be much more costly to handle. This seems reasonable. So, perhaps Social Security is just fine.

Yet others are projecting serious problems as early as 2020, calling for changes such as Speaker of the House Paul Ryan's proposal to change price indexing from being attached to cost of living and attach them to wage increases. Essentially, wages increase more slowly in percentage terms, and benefits would be reduced in the long term.

The arguments are confusing and policy wonks could have a joyful debate over these things for the next ten thousand years without reaching an understandable conclusion. We can simplify it. Here are the major points to consider:

- There are more of us living longer.
- The current revenue levels are challenged by the growth of benefits, no matter the reason for that growth.
- A significant amount of the wealth that is generated in this country is not tapped for supporting old-age and disability.

The first corollary to Immutable Law of Human Organizations states that when the issue becomes attaining and maintaining power, corruption will always ensue, and it may take many forms because people are devious. Despite all the decent, professional, and caring people who say we have 2.85 trillion dollars sitting there to support the system, we do not. What we have is a lot of papers sitting in Parkersburg, West Virginia that say they can be redeemed for 2.85 trillion dollars. The problem is we have to redeem them from our federal government. They do not have the money and can only produce it through increased taxes or increased deficit.

As a population that believes everyone has an inherent right to "Life, Liberty, and the pursuit of Happiness," what do we expect Social Security to accomplish?

First point: There are more of us and we are living longer

When I was in college in the early 1970s, a fellow by the name of Paul Ehrlich wrote a very popular and successful book called *The Population Bomb*. I recall glancing through it, agreeing with its premise, and setting it aside to pursue issues more closely related to the now. I did not dismiss it, nor did I pursue it. It was a problem for later.

Today, population is not tomorrow's problem for the world. Let's look at the population for the world from the year 1900 to today and consider the projections for halfway through this century.

YEAR	WORLD POPULATION
1900	1,600,000,000
2018	7,632, 819,325
2050	9,700,000,000

In less than a century and a half we expect that the world population will have grown so that wherever there was one person in 1900, there will be slightly over six people standing. The United States is experiencing a lower growth rate than, for example, India, China, and many other developing countries. Our story is much the same, with a current population estimated at 326,200,000 and a projected 480,000,000 by 2050. This is a total growth of approximately 47%.

However, growth has been and will for the foreseeable future remain on an upward curve. The metric for the United States from now to mid-century is an increase of slightly over 48%, or roughly one and a half people where we now have one.

In many ways our overall health is improving, thus enhancing longevity prospects. For example, according to a report from the Center for Disease Control, smoking is the leading cause of preventable disease and death in the United States, accounting for more than 480,000 every year, or one in five deaths.

An estimated 36.5 million adults in the United States currently smoke cigarettes. More than 16 million Americans live with a smoking-related disease. In 2015, about 15 of every 100 adults aged 18 years or older (15.1%) currently smoked cigarettes. This is a decline from 21 out of 100 (20.9%) in 2005.

Medicine has advanced greatly in the last fifty years in understanding the human body, defining the root causes of many diseases and developing cures and vaccines. Even cancer is slowly giving ground to our drive to make it a thing of the past. In another fifty years, we will look back to today and be amazed at how little we knew about health and making it happen. This transition will take place faster and more effectively if we adopt universal health care.

If we do not blow up the planet with nuclear missiles or suffer any of the other eight or nine scenarios for planet-wide devastation, then there will be a lot more of us on Social Security. It really is that simple. The time to correct the problems with Social Security is now.

Second point: Current revenue for social security is being outpaced by growth

The history of Social Security revenue has been that in most years the revenue has exceeded the required distributions. That excess revenue is supposed to be set aside to cover any revenue shortfalls in succeeding years. That has worked well enough for most of the life of Social Security.

However, in 2010 there was a gap where required disbursements were higher than revenues. This gap was covered by excess revenue that was available from previous years. The gap has grown larger with each succeeding year. It appears likely that by the year 2020, the gap will exceed the available excess revenues.

This means several things are already happening and will happen:

- President Trump's proposed budget, recently released, includes cuts to Social Security and Medicare. Conservatives will try to cut the required disbursements, if not immediately then for the future.

- The blame game will continue to accelerate. This includes, but is not limited to, labeling Social Security disbursements as "entitlements" and calling the checks Social Security benefits. Who can object to reducing entitlements and scaling back benefits? After all, those things are actually charity. In reality, they are not.

They are insurance payments from an insurance program we were required to pay into for all of our working life, with the understanding that the government would hold it for us and then pay it back when we retired and needed it. Further steps in the blame game will likely include increased medical costs, which cannot be avoided unless Universal Health Care is implemented and costs are controlled.

People will also blame tightening requirements, cutting coverage, and virtually non-existent cheating for increasing the costs.

This will work. It has worked in blaming illegal voting to justify voter registration laws. In an August 16, 2014, article for *The Washington Post*, Loyola Law School Professor Justin Levitt, who was currently on leave at the time of the article to work with the Department of Justice to oversee voting, wrote that he has been tracking allegations of voter fraud for years, including any "credible allegation that someone may have pretended to be someone else at the polls, in any way that an ID law could fix." "So far," he wrote, "I've found about 31 different incidents (some of which involve multiple ballots) since 2000, anywhere in the country. To put this in perspective, the 31 incidents below come in the context of general, primary, special, and municipal elections from 2000 through 2014. In general and primary elections alone, more than 1 billion ballots were cast in that period."

Many states passed restrictive voter identification acts and reduced voting hours at key voting stations, despite the obvious non-existence of voter fraud by individual voters.

- No acknowledgement of the 2020 problem will be made, since such acknowledgement would "open a can of worms" as to how this situation came about and lead to an acknowledgement of the ongoing "legal" con game which has been carried out since Social Security was first implemented.

- The problem of "more of us, living longer" noted above will be used to persuade younger voters that there are too few of them and it is unfair for them to have to pay for older people who should have "planned better." The real issue here is that the suppression of wage growth for the poor and middle class has simply reduced the pot from which Social Security revenue is derived. There are plenty of workers, just not plenty of wages. Besides, the Social Security and Disability Trust fund have $2.85 trillion in them, which should be more than adequate to cover everyone currently on Social Security and Medicare. This means that today's workers are simply putting aside money to be returned to them when they retire.

- As 2020 is a presidential election year, the disbursements will continue without pause or public acknowledgement of any problem. How will this be managed when there is an insufficiency in revenue that is not covered by previous excess revenue? Simple. As required by law and as envisioned from Social Security's beginning, they will draw from the Social Security and Disability Trust Funds. Oops! How can we cash special obligation bonds payable only by the United States government if they have no actual cash set aside for this purpose? The first thing that will not happen is setting or increasing any tax for this purpose. It is, after all, a presidential election year. We cannot upset the voters and have any hope of retaining office, which is the only real reason we take any action. The second thing is the only other option. The bonds will be quietly redeemed, and the deficit will grow. Who could have any problem with that? Conservative policy in real life is to scream about the deficit if they are not in power and ignore and increase the deficit if they are in power. Simple. The time to correct the problems with Social Security is now.

Third Point: A significant amount of the wealth that is generated in this country is not tapped for supporting old age and disability

My most recent information as of this writing is that the payroll tax, FICA, does not tax over $127,000. It is not an easy calculation to determine what is truly fair, so consider this a first pass at the problem.

- In 2011, the Social Security Administration reported Total Earned Income was 12.95 trillion dollars ($12,950,000,000,000).

- In 2011, the Social Security Administration reported Total Disbursement for Social Security and related Programs by the Social Security 738.4 billion dollars ($738,400,000,000).

- Simple math, dividing 738,400,000,000 by 12,950,000,000,000, indicates that only 5.7% of earned income is paid into FICA, while 94.3% does not contribute to supporting the old and disabled. All earned income that is not assessed is over the cap of $127,000.

There is no justification for this cap other than if you are rich enough, you do not have to pay.

These figures are from 2011, but it is doubtful that there have been any significant changes in the percentages. Why is it that a program structured for everyone is paid for by so few?

When President Roosevelt worked to make Social Security a federal program, many questions were raised as to whether it was even constitutional. There was significant opposition to Social Security. In part, President Roosevelt as able to sell the program because it was structured in a way as to not significantly affect the wealthy and large corporations.

The real question is, why should we allow such an unequal situation to continue today if we are truly committed to the inalienable rights of every person to "Life, Liberty, and the Pursuit of Happiness"? We should not. As a society, we are a team. As a team, all members must contribute to all things on an equitable basis. If you have more, this is not a reason for a special indulgence so you can contribute a lesser percentage to the need. The time to correct the problems with Social Security is now.

Fourth Point: The first Corollary to the Immutable Law of Human Organizations states: when the issue becomes attaining and maintaining power, corruption will ensue...

Dear Reader,

The Law of Human Organizations is not pretty good. It is not mostly accurate. It is not a nice guideline. It is immutable. As the thesaurus notes, alternative words for immutable are: unchallengeable, absolute, not able to be forfeited, unassailable, incontrovertible, indisputable and undeniable. The first corollary is the only outcome there can be. The only factors affecting the first corollary are time, opportunity, and vaccinations.

The United States government has been operating for two hundred and thirty years. The Social Security program has been operating for eighty-two years. Although the Constitution gives us the ability to vaccinate and limit power and corruption, we have been extremely remiss in doing so.

There has been ample time and opportunity to attain power and alter the organization to retain power and make fortunes that King Midas would envy. The story of king Midas is a myth about a man so desirous of wealth that he wished everything he touched would turn to gold. His wish was granted. He touched his daughter. Things did not end well.

The corruption that has affected our government has taken many forms in the pursuit of wealth. Social Security, although not intended to be so, has been one of the most devious.

The plan was simple. Pay into an insurance fund. When you retire, receive payments to assist your livelihood. Not everyone who pays in will live to retirement. Not everyone who retires will live very long. As long as the money is set aside, the fund will grow and everyone will prosper.

Enter the First Corollary. It is impossible to establish a fund and fill it with large sums of money intended to be spent only for a specific reason and allow access to it by a bunch of politicians. They will immutably raid it.

The Social Security Administration, echoed by many politicians, states very clearly, you could make a case: "In this indirect sense, one could say that the Social Security Trust Funds are being spent for non-Social Security purposes."

It is hard to believe that this was not an excellent con job from the beginning by those seeking power and money. In fairness, it must be noted that the bond was created by an amendment to Liberty Bonds. Those bonds helped fund WWII and were righteously paid off when the time came.

This was done relatively easily due to the post-war economic boom. In the sixties, President Lyndon B. Johnson negotiated an increase in the rate of the FICA tax. The Social Security Fund grew. Special obligation bonds continued. FICA money remained in the General Fund rather than being set aside. Spending grew apace.

The politicians had a ready-made con. They did not need to create one. They merrily spent the funds.

The government is now referring to our Social Security checks as a "Federal Benefit Payment." This is not a benefit; it is our money paid out of our earned income! Not only did we all contribute to Social Security, but our employers did too. It totaled 15% of our income before taxes.

If you averaged $30,000 per year over your working life, that is close to $180,000 invested in Social Security. If you calculate the future value of your monthly investment in Social Security ($375/month, including both your and your employers' contributions) at a meager 1% interest rate compounded monthly, after 40 years of working you would have more than 1.3 million dollars saved.

This is your personal investment. Upon retirement, if you took out only

3% per year, you would receive $39,318 per year, or $3,277 per month. That is almost three times more than today's average Social Security benefit of $1,230 per month, according to the Social Security Administration. And your retirement fund would last more than 33 years (until you are 98 if you retire at age 65). I can only imagine how much better most average-income people could live in retirement if our government had just invested our money in low-risk interest-earning accounts. Just because they borrowed the money does not mean that our investments were a charity! The time to correct the problems with Social Security is now!

Fifth Point: The fact that, despite the really decent, professional, and caring people who say we have $2.85 trillion dollars sitting around to support the system, we do not. What we have is a lot of papers sitting in Parkersburg, West Virginia that say they can be redeemed for $2.85 trillion dollars. The problem is, we have to redeem the money from our federal government and they do not have the money and can only produce it through an increase in taxes and the deficit.

$2.85 trillion dollars is roughly three years of total disbursements at the estimated 2016 total disbursement of $928.9 billion dollars. That is a significant sum and demonstrates that the original plan for sustaining the system was sound. For eighty-two years the disbursements have been made in a timely fashion, and people have received their payment from the insurance fund into which they had been required to pay.

As noted above, the Social Security system appears poised to fray, beginning as early as 2020. Therefore, the question is, what should we do to prevent the system from going essentially bankrupt, or the system being fully funded from General Revenue, the clear intent when the special obligation bonds started to be utilized, inflicting tremendous stress on the General Operating Budget?

Those are the two alternatives. The first is to allow the Social Security system to go bankrupt and not meet its obligations, or reduce those obligations so it can get by with less. This is the purpose of efforts to set a higher number of years for eligibility and of labeling disbursements as government benefits. Those actions are not intended to be as mean-spirited and uncaring as they appear. Instead they are a desperate effort from people who do not want to be in office when the dam breaks.

The second alternative is to cash in the special obligation bonds and pay for them out of General Fund Revenues. This could be done on an annualized basis by only cashing in sufficient bonds to cover the gap each year, which will likely have to begin in 2020, or by cashing the bonds at a faster rate and creating a reserve which contains actual cash.

There are problems with either scenario. An annualized basis is likely to increase in size every year as there are more retirees that are living longer. It also begs the question how many current recipients have been shorted over the years as part of the con; the reason for the "entitlements" labeling. In recent history, my wife and I saw no increase in our checks in 2015, 2016, or 2017. The increase in 2018 may be described as minimal if you wish to be offensively kind in your description.

The special obligation bonds will have to be cashed in and whichever option is chosen, annualized or accelerated withdrawal, the money is going to come from us. The real question is which of us and how? Again, there are choices for identifying the funding.

1. Fund through increasing the deficit

Also known as kicking the can down the track, simply increasing the deficit as even a temporary solution seems less than desirable. If you loan a guy $1,000 because he is $5,000 in debt and a year later he asks for another $1,000 because he is $20,000 in debt, will you loan him the money? Will you loan it at the same interest rate? How many years will you be willing to do this?

Remember, the special obligation bonds are our obligation. The deficit, also is our obligation. Do you recall something about robbing Peter to pay Paul.

2. Cut other expenditures to free up funds to pay for the bonds

But what will be cut? Whether you think we should cut social programs you do not approve of, aid to other countries, or defense spending, there are consequences that will not sit well with a significant part of our population. For example, cutting defense spending could release tremendous funds to offset the special obligation bonds and we could still spend way more than the next seven countries combined.

That position would be adamantly opposed by those who believe our defense spending is vital to the defense of our homeland, especially those in the military industrial complex who make billions of dollars off the defense budget.

There are those who would support this position because they do not believe this spending at this level actually defends us. They would note that in seventy years the United States has not won a war, but we've never lost one either. We have called it a draw and still have to man the border; we have declared victory and walked away several times without having achieved any lasting peace, and we are still fighting our longest war. Any place you think should be cut would create the same type of division in our country. There is little doubt that we should work at better, rational decision-making in our spending on every issue, but this will not happen unless we pass the amendment to the constitution to change the way our government operates. Solving one problem by creating others is unlikely to prove satisfactory.

3. Raise more revenue to pay for the bonds

We are talking here about taking money out of our pockets. This solution is known as time to pay the piper. But there are many decisions left to make, like who should pay, how much, and how we should use that money.

The first and easiest step is to eliminate the cap on earned income that allows people to contribute, from those who are well off to those who are bonkers rich. Everyone must be made to pay a fair share. We can still allow everyone to receive Social Security when they retire, but we can place an appropriate cap on the point when what they contribute engenders increased payback beyond the need to accomplish what the program is intended for. We will discuss this further in the next section. A fair share from everyone under these conditions would be an equitable way to support the team. Without changing the percentage on FICA tax, this would generate a tremendous amount of revenue to operate Social Security now and in the future. Combined with universal health care it would provide funds to cash in the special obligation bonds and return benefits to current retirees that they should have received over the years.

The winning point of paying off the special obligation bonds (our obligation) this way is we do not penalize ourselves in any other way.

The sixth point is: As a population who believes everyone has a right to "Life, Liberty, and the pursuit of Happiness" what should we expect Social Security to accomplish?

The Social Security Act was signed into law by President Roosevelt on August 14, 1935. In addition to several provisions for general welfare, the new act created a social insurance program designed to pay retired workers aged sixty-five years or older a continuing income after retirement. The act laid the groundwork for the modern welfare system in the United States, with its primary purpose to provide aid for the elderly, the disabled, the unemployed, and children.

We must remember that a key element of the introduction to the Constitution of the United States is " . . . to promote the general welfare . . ."

Social Security is not an entitlement. Social Security is not a benefit. Social Security is not something being grabbed by "takers." Social Security is simply an insurance payment from a fund we have all contributed to, which was established to promote the general welfare.

A list of the things we might want to accomplish with Social Security, includes:

- Provision of a responsible monthly payment that will enable recipients to maintain a level of living above the poverty level. This amount should be calculated using an accurate model of the expenditure necessary to maintain that level for recipients. Strong arguments have been made that the CPI index is not an accurate model for this use. This will likely require higher disbursements to recipients. Keep in mind that very little of the money received in Social Security disbursements goes into savings accounts. It is spent for maintaining a level of living that is too often below the level of poverty. But it is spent in our economy. Increasing payments puts more money into our economy and boosts economic growth, unlike for instance, huge tax breaks for corporations which are not reinvested in jobs and production in our country.

- Provision of adequate medical care that will enable recipients to maintain a level of health as positively as possible. This would be more easily accomplished by the implementation of universal health care, even if Medicare is used as the base model for such care. The costs would then be shifted out of Social Security into a separate program and eliminate the needs on one side becoming stressors on the other side. Medicare costs would increase so payments from Social Security for Medicare diminish or completely offset increases in the Social Security disbursement.

- Provision of assistance for the elderly, disabled, and families with children for housing so they have a safe and reasonably comfortable accommodation without having to sacrifice sustenance, clothing or medical needs, or vice versa.

- Restoration of the Social Security Fund and the Disability Fund to a cash basis, with a true "lockbox" preventing the utilization of those funds for anything other than its intended purpose. House Speaker Paul Ryan has used the concept of a "lockbox" to protect future FICA tax collections, however he envisions much smaller protections, much smaller disbursements, and no cashing in of the special obligation bonds. It is integral to any solution for this crisis that the funds be limited to the purpose for which they are collected and not be diverted to other purposes by special obligation bonds or any other ploy Congress might attempt to implement.

The refund should be paid for by everyone with a surcharge placed on the FICA Tax until refund is completed, as follows:

FICA Tax Surcharge Assessment Schedule

Earned Income	Percentage Assessment	Amount paid on maximum earned level	Accumulated maximum paid at maximum earned level
0 — 20,000	0.5%	$100	$100
20,001 — 50,000	2%	$400	$500
50,001 — 100,000	2.3%	$1,150	$1,650
100,001 — 150,000	2.5%	$1,250	$2,900
150,001 — 200,000	3%	$1,500	$4,400
200,001 — 250,000	4%	$2,000	$6,400
250,001 — 450,000	5%	$10,000	$16,400
450,001 — 750,000	7.5%	$150,000	$38,900
750,001 — 1,000,000	9%	$100,000	$138,900
1,000,001 — 2,000,000	10%	$150,000	$188,900
2,000,001 — 3,000,000	15%	$200,000	$388,900
3,000,001 — 4,000,000	20%	$400,000	$788,900
4,000,001 — 5,000,000	20%	$400,000	$1,388,900

Add 20% ($400,000) to the Accumulated Maximum per each additional $1,000,000

A tax on all revenue is not counted as earned income on the same schedule as earned income. Social Security disbursements, Veterans Administration disbursements, and child support payments should be exempt from this, whether from government or private sources. There should be tax of ninety percent on all money housed outside of the United States, unless within a year of the passage of this amendment the money is accurately reported to the IRS and all other taxes that would be paid on earned income, plus the required amount for the repayment to the Social Security Funds is paid per the schedule of payments for the repayment. All corporations shall pay ten percent on gross earnings, including earnings credited outside of the United States. All employers shall pay five percent of their total payroll for the year, including bonuses or any other cash disbursements.

- An annual increase on payments of three percent plus the increase in CPI to ensure Social Security stays level with the actual cost of living.

- An annual increase of five percent on payments as a repayment of the funds placed into special obligation bonds. This annual increase shall continue until fifty percent of the outstanding bonds have been redeemed. At that point the bonds should be continued to be redeemed until they all have been converted to actual money and placed in a lockbox reserve account, which can not be accessed for any other purpose than the operation of the Social Security system.

- Maximum payout should be calculated as equivalent to the amount paid in by the current $127,000 limit, adjusted for inflation.

AMENDMENT TO THE CONSTITUTION TO PROTECT AND PRESERVE SOCIAL SECURITY

1.1 The cap on earned income at which the FICA Tax is no longer assessed shall be eliminated. There shall also be no cap on the assessment of corporate payroll taxes to the corporation.

1.2 The Social Security Fund and the Disability Fund shall be restored to a cash basis, with a true "lockbox" preventing the utilization of those funds for any other purpose than the administration of the Social Security System.

1.3 The payment for restoring the funds shall be paid for by everyone with a surcharge placed on the FICA Tax until repayment is completed, as outlined in the **FICA Tax Surcharge Assessment Schedule** *noted above.*

1.4 At the rate of five percent per year the restored funds shall be paid to recipients until such time as fifty percent of the special obligation bonds have been redeemed. These payments shall become a permanent increase to the payments. These increases in Social Security disbursements shall not be considered in determining pay raises for Congress. The bonds shall be continued to be redeemed until the Social Security System is completely operated on a cash basis. No interest shall be paid on the cash reserve unless a projected shortfall indicates a need to replenish the reserve to protect the system. In that instance, a surcharge shall be added to the collections to replenish the reserve.

1.5 An annual increase on payments to beneficiaries of three percent plus the increase in CPI to ensure Social Security stays level with the actual cost of living shall be made.

1.6 The retirement age for Social security shall be 65 years old.

1.7 The purpose of the Social Security Program shall be to enable recipients as a group the ability to maintain living above the poverty level for the elderly, the disabled, and children in terms of food, shelter, and medical care.

A FINAL APPEAL

"Eternal vigilance is the price of liberty."

— Thomas Paine 1777

We have what should be the greatest country in the world. It is not, and it will end if we continue on the path we have been following. No Congress, no president, no court can change this path. They have neither the will nor the strength to overcome the distortion of our government's structure that has allowed all of this to happen. We, and only 'we' have that strength. The question is, do we have the will to become the country our founders envisioned?

I titled this book *UBUNTU: I Am Because We Are* to emphasize the fact that teamwork is the foundation of being human. I explored the innate structure of teams and its tremendous impact in allowing human beings to dominate this planet. I shed some light on the built-in weakness, namely, individuals and groups ignoring their fellow citizens for their own gain. I reviewed the reasons team is how *we* reached were *we* are. I have declared the situation immutable. We can't make it different. It is what we are. Only we can make it work, so we can all share equally in the right to Life, Liberty, and the Pursuit of Happiness. If some do not have these rights, then none may honestly claim to have them.

The amendments described in this book are what I believe are necessary for our country to be restored to the correct path and to ensure government is run by the consent of the governed. These proposals will likely require fine-tuning. They will most certainly require an intense and lengthy struggle to achieve. Again, I do not claim to have all the answers, but I know that we can either live or perish together as a nation.

The meaning of *Ubuntu* presents a whole answer to any chance there may be for all of *we* to exist peacefully. You may disagree with some or all of the solutions I suggest to regain control of the direction of our country. That is fine. All I ask you to do is grab hold of each other's hands, search together for solutions to these very real and overwhelming difficult issues that may destroy us all, and let us cross the finish line together shouting *UBUNTU*!

ACKNOWLEDGEMENTS

Writing is a challenging and demanding task to undertake. Hint for you would-be writers out there, writing is correctly defined as re-writing, followed by re-writing. What level of good writing I may have achieved was supported by the following, among others: Betsy Ashton, Edith Johnson, Edna G. Whittier, Rodney Franklin, Judy Ailytz, Joe Fournier, and my ever-patient wife, Nancy Wheeler. Thank you all!

ABOUT THE AUTHOR

For his service as a U.S. Army Infantry Combat Platoon Leader during the Vietnam war, John Koelsch received a Bronze Star w. "V" Device for Valor, 2 Purple Hearts, and a Combat Infantryman's Badge. '*UBUNTU*: I Am Because We Are' a peaceful treatise on fixing the fractured state of American governance is his first non-fiction book and the result of over three decades of service in the public sector and earning a Bachelors degree in political science. Since 1993, his writing, which includes poetry, short fiction and flash fiction has been awarded numerous awards including the 2015 Meringoff Writing Award in Non-Fiction. He was a semi-finalist for the Panther Creek Non-Fiction Book Awards and has received multiple awards for his participation in the National Veterans Creative Arts Festival. Seven of his short stories and thirteen of his individual poems have been published. To learn more about John and his work visit his website www.johnkoelsch.com

Made in the USA
Lexington, KY
16 November 2019

57105428R00109